ISBN 978-0-428-14312-1
PIBN 11249067

This book is a reproduction of an important historical work. Forgotten Books uses
state-of-the-art technology to digitally reconstruct the work, preserving the original format
whilst repairing imperfections present in the aged copy. In rare cases, an imperfection in
the original, such as a blemish or missing page, may be replicated in our edition. We do,
however, repair the vast majority of imperfections successfully; any imperfections that
remain are intentionally left to preserve the state of such historical works.

1 MONTH OF
FREE
READING

at
www.ForgottenBooks.com

By purchasing this book you are eligible for one month membership to ForgottenBooks.com, giving you unlimited access to our entire collection of over 1,000,000 titles via our web site and mobile apps.

To claim your free month visit:
www.forgottenbooks.com/free1249067

English
Français
Deutsche
Italiano
Español
Português

www.forgottenbooks.com

Mythology Photography **Fiction**
Fishing Christianity **Art** Cooking
Essays Buddhism Freemasonry
Medicine **Biology** Music **Ancient
Egypt** Evolution Carpentry Physics
Dance Geology **Mathematics** Fitness
Shakespeare **Folklore** Yoga Marketing
Confidence Immortality Biographies
Poetry **Psychology** Witchcraft
Electronics Chemistry History **Law**
Accounting **Philosophy** Anthropology
Alchemy Drama Quantum Mechanics
Atheism Sexual Health **Ancient History**
Entrepreneurship Languages Sport
Paleontology Needlework Islam
Metaphysics Investment Archaeology
Parenting Statistics Criminology
Motivational

o

Historic, archived document

Do not assume content reflects current
scientific knowledge, policies, or practices.

CROPS AND MARKETS

Published Weekly by the
United States Department of Agriculture

CERTIFICATE: By direction of the Secretary of Agriculture the matter contained herein is published as statistical information and is required for the proper transaction of the public business. Free distribution is limited to copies "necessary in the transaction of public business required by law." Subscription price $1 per year (foreign rate $2) payable in cash or money order to the Superintendent of Documents, Government Printing Office, Washington, D. C.

WASHINGTON, D. C.   MARCH 22, 1924.   VOL. 1, No. 12

Index to this Issue.

	Page.
Livestock, Meats, and Wool	178
Fruits and Vegetables	181
Dairy and Poultry	184
Hay	185
Grain	186
Feed	188
Seeds	189
Cotton	190
Foreign Crops and Markets	192

Review.

Prices on all classes of livestock were lowered at Chicago during the week March 10-15. The disproportionate manner in which cattle runs arrived assisted killers in effecting a 25-75¢ decline on lower grades of fed steers early in the period, approximately half of the week's receipts arriving on Monday.

Finishers continued to take all grades of steers suitable for further finishing. Increased receipts of hogs coincident with contracted shipping demand were bearish factors. Expanded country loadings of lambs gave buyers an opportunity to force price reductions, while fat sheep were also lowered. Finishers and shearers remained active, displaying confidence in future market prices.

Reduced receipts of fresh meats were accompanied by a fair response in the way of price advances. Consumptive demand was not materially increased but lighter offerings placed sellers in a position to hold and in most instances to advance prices.

Butter markets were barely steady. Trading lacks snap and is mostly for current requirements only. Production trend is uncertain. Imports were light, but heavy shipments are expected early in April.

Primary cheese markets were more active, with trading on a more confident basis, but distributing markets were irregular, with business on the whole dull. Buyers are apparently waiting for it to be more definitely established that prices are at low point.

Exports of apples continue fairly heavy, according to reports of the International Apple Shippers' Association. To March 8, aggregate movement to foreign markets was two-thirds greater than last season, totaling 2,840,000 barrels and 4,514,000 boxes. Some of these shipments were from Canada, but most from the United States. New York has now become the leading shipping State, many of the smaller-size New York apples entering into export trade. More than 600 carloads from all parts of the country arrived in New York City during the week March 10-15, and the market was rather slow. Northwestern Extra Fancy Winesaps strengthened at Washington

91020°—24—1

shipping points. Total March 1 apple holdings in cold storage were about 50% larger than those of a year ago and 83% above the five-year average, with but three months remaining in the active season. Jobbing prices for old cabbage declined further during the week, and considerable stock of inferior quality was offered. New cabbage was moving from the South at the rate of 100 cars per day, compared with only 30 a year ago. The Chicago potato market sagged under heavy arrivals, with an average of 260 cars on track each day. Northern round whites declined in that city and at shipping points. The Idaho potato situation, however, was much brighter, and considerably higher prices were being received. Celery and lettuce markets made sharp advances. At some points, western lettuce gained as much as $1.50 per crate. Asparagus was coming from California in larger volume, but the Florida strawberry season is fast waning. The week's shipments of 16 products decreased to 13,240 cars.

Hay market was stronger. Inadequate receipts of good hay caused a slight reaction from recent downward trend. First cutting of alfalfa in Arizona is expected next month. Best grades of alfalfa and prairie were in good demand from dairymen and feeders.

Larger farm reserves than generally expected weakened the grain market. Wheat suffers heaviest decline. Demand for corn shows some reduction and supplies in markets slightly larger. Oats were relatively firmer than other grains. Flax market was weakened by foreign importations.

Feed markets were weak as a result of accumulation of supplies and a light demand from important feeding and dairy sections. Corn feeds were quiet and prices held barely steady. Oil meals, too, showed a weaker tendency. Production of all feedstuffs was ample. The movement was good.

Prices of clover and alfalfa seeds advanced during the week March 10-15 with the increased demand for these seeds. In many sections the soil is still a little wet for sowing, so more activity is expected in the seed business as the soil dries out. Many seedmen are offering 1922 seed corn because of better germination than their 1923 corn.

Cotton prices advanced during the week March 10-15, under the influence of reports of further delay in farm work in the south, due to unfavorable weather, of more settled labor conditions in the English cotton spinning centers, and of a larger consumption of cotton in February than was generally expected by the trade. The price of No. 5 or Middling spot cotton in 10 designated markets, advanced 82 points, closing at 29.28¢ per lb. March future contracts at New York closed at 28.95¢ on the 15th, compared with 27.95¢ on the 8th. March futures at New Orleans closed at 29.50¢ compared with 28.78¢ on the 8th.

177

Livestock - Meats - Wool

Prices of Livestock Fell.

All species of livestock at Chicago took a price tumble of varying degrees during the week ended March 15. The disproportionate manner in which cattle runs arrived assisted killers in effecting a 25–75¢ decline on lower grades of fed steers early in the period, approximately half of the week's receipts arriving on Monday. But small runs later turned the tables and week-end sessions saw most of the downturn restored. Finishers continued to take all grades of steers suitable for further finish, paying particular attention to meaty selected offerings, the price future of which looks dependable providing too many are not put on feed.

Hogs were compelled to surrender prices scored a week earlier when butchers were the highest of the year so far. Increased receipts coincident with contracted shipping demand were bearish factors which were further aggravated by the cautious and indifferent attitude of. big killers. Butchers averaging 180 lbs. upward sold within a very narrow spread and, while heavies continued to command a slight premium at Chicago, 200 pounders often realized the top at St. Louis. Receipts ran about 10 per cent larger than a year earlier and plainly were too large for trade requirements. Knowing the delicate sympathy between future prices and receipts, the volume of which can not be known with accuracy, trade prophets were unusually wary and, so many prognostications having been discredited recently, noncommittal. Pork loins advanced sharply in Chicago and light loins there at $16–$17 looked high as contrasted with a $7.45 top on butchers at the close and an average of approximately $7.25 for the week.

Fat lambs, too, fell from their high price estate of a week earlier. At Chicago an early top of $16.65 was obsolete at the close, when $16 was the high mark. Expanded country loadings, representing in good measure the anxiety of western finishers to get their wares through the market gate at the year's most remunerative prices, gave buyers a chance to use the price lash. Such an opportunity has infrequently been presented during the last month and was regarded by most members of the trade as only temporary, the statistical position of fat lambs continuing a strong one. Fat sheep weakened too, and with warm weather approaching, a seasonal run of grass sheep from the southwest impending that class has probably passed its peak price era for the season. Before the drop, however, fat handyweight ewes advanced to $11, shorn kinds making $9.25 at Chicago. Displaying confidence in future price markets, finishers and shearers remained active, and consequently the spread between fat and shearing lambs narrowed, lambs going to the country for a short turn and for shearing purposes upward to $15.60 at Chicago, when killers there were refusing to exceed $16 for best fat offerings.

Fed steers and yearlings of value to sell at and above $10.50 did not feel the downturn imposed on lower grades, the relative scarcity of the former providing a price support. But under $10.50 and especially under $9.50 unevenness and lethargy was pronounced, a liberal share of the fat steer contingent being of value to cash at $8.25–$10. At Chicago practically nothing averaging 1,000 lbs. or more had to sell under $7.75 at the close. Big weight steers topped repeatedly at $12, a price which was no higher than recently, although bullocks at that figure had often seen a shorter ration on corn than the $12 steers a week or more earlier. The fed steer run included a moderate quota of heavy offerings eligible to $11–$11.75, long yearlings at the outside figure being the highest priced youngsters since January. Long yearlings, including a few heifers, sold upward to $11.60, but most mixed yearlings were $7.75–$9.75 kinds. Fat steers of value to sell above $11 continued to display gross margins of profit amounting to $3–$4, and often comparable upturns were registered by all weights selling below $10, although as a rule smaller but at the same time moderately liberal profits were generally presented by steers selling under $10.50.

Inspired by the way heavy bullocks are selling, finishers, paying for a short turn, paid upward to $9.75 for 1,179-lb. half-fat offerings at Omaha; Mineral Point, Wis., grass finishers paying upward to $9 for 1,100-lb. steers at Chicago, where numerous qualitied beefy steers went out at $8–$8.50. The bulk of stockers and feeders turned at $6–$7.25, however, at Chicago, a spread of $6.25–$7.50 taking the bulk at Kansas City. Fewer stockers and feeders have gone out so far this year than a year earlier. At the same time marketings have been

on a parity with a year ago. The movement of southwestern grass fat cattle is expected to be smaller than a year ago, a factor which should prove bullish on lower grades of native grass fat steers and she stock during May and June. Western coast buyers during the week under review were active at Denver and other intermountain markets, taking heavy fat steers and cows. Efforts to depress she stock at Chicago were fruitless, beef heifers especially selling actively at $6.25–$7.75 mostly. Too many common and medium grade, light-weight vealers arrived and the spread between these and selected 130–160-lb. averages became unusually wide, the former selling largely at $8–$8.50, while shippers paid upward to $13 for the latter.

Receipts, Shipments, and Local Slaughter.

Week March 10-15, 1924, with Comparisons.

Market.	Cattle and calves.[1]			Hogs.			Sheep.		
	Receipts.	Shipments.	Local slaughter.	Receipts.	Shipments.	Local slaughter.	Receipts.	Shipments.	Local slaughter.
Chicago........	71,735	20,728	51,007	224,152	59,601	164,461	73,079	24,414	40,565
Denver [2]......	7,291	4,050	2,450	11,398	1,339	11,043	39,548	37,816	4,145
East St. Louis..	14,546	4,448	9,120	92,988	47,274	34,138	6,946	446	6,568
Fort Worth.....	11,881	3,209	6,309	11,435	1,164	9,255	8,115	1,871	896
Indianapolis...	8,606	3,707	4,716	44,635	17,752	27,184	1,264	231	1,033
Kansas City....	33,892	12,844	21,328	57,092	23,248	34,124	24,027	4,106	18,677
Oklahoma City	4,396	2,404	3,078	5,142	1,858	4,838	36	130	36
Omaha.........	35,450	15,048	30,344	106,188	26,811	79,287	47,396	12,222	33,491
St. Joseph [1]..	12,622	4,537	7,815	45,921	14,126	31,177	22,509	4,929	18,692
St. Paul [2]....	22,024	4,419	16,142	83,503	20,257	65,419	3,256	556	1,333
Sioux City.....	15,658	7,424	7,191	100,102	51,210	43,978	2,812	1,397	1,334
Wichita [1].....	6,204	3,356	1,729	15,686	989	15,564	423	....	422
Total.........	243,655	86,171	151,229	799,642	265,366	521,366	225,514	88,168	136,192
Total Mar. 3-8, 1924........	237,320	76,802	156,946	728,471	243,389	515,532	202,638	72,938	118,348
Total Mar. 12-17, 1923...	229,425	79,562	146,507	734,819	186,665	539,914	212,077	65,502	138,584

[1] Movement of calves Mar. 10-15: Receipts, 50,760; shipments, 9,573; local slaughter, 42,370.
[2] Week ending Friday, Mar. 14.

Daily Average Weight and Cost of Hogs.

Week March 10-15, 1924, with Comparisons.

	Chicago.		East St. Louis.		Fort Worth.		Kansas City.		Omaha.		St. Paul.	
	Wt.	Cost.	Wt.	Cost.	Wt.	Cost.	Wt.	Cost.	Wt.	Cost.	Wt.	Cost
	Lbs.	Per 100 lbs.	Lbs.	Per 100 lbs.	Lbs.	Per 100 lbs.	Lbs.	Per 100 lbs.	Lbs.	Per 100 lbs.	Lbs.	Per 100 lbs.
Monday..............	242	$7.46	217	$7.45	185	$6.65	229	$7.04	244	$6.99	208	$6.94
Tuesday.............	236	7.48	217	7.48	182	6.74	225	7.10	247	7.08	216	7.05
Wednesday........	240	7.37	218	7.41	182	6.76	225	7.08	245	7.00	227	6.96
Thursday..........	232	7.29	208	7.27	188	6.78	236	6.98	248	6.95	218	6.96
Friday.............	235	7.20	231	7.23	166	6.43	226	6.95	248	6.86	217	6.85
Saturday...........	244	7.22	209	7.33	192	6.29	217	6.93	250	6.95	205	6.84
Average:												
Mar. 10-15, 1924..	238	7.35	217	7.37	185	6.70	227	7.03	247	6.98	217	6.95
Mar. 3-8, 1924......	235	7.34	215	7.29	191	6.85	231	6.95	242	6.97	214	6.95
Mar. 12-17, 1923...	240	8.22	201	8.39	184	7.78	221	8.01	254	7.90	217	7.94

The above prices are computed on packer and shipper purchases.

Weights and Prices of Stocker and Feeder Steers at Chicago.

Week March 10-15, 1924, with Comparisons.

Weight range.	Number of head.			Per cent of total by weight ranges.			Average weight (pounds).			Average price per 100 pounds.		
	Week Mar. 10-15, 1924.	Week Mar. 3-8, 1924.	Week Mar. 12-17, 1923.	Week Mar. 10-15, 1924.	Week Mar. 3-8, 1924.	Week Mar. 12-17, 1923.	Week Mar. 10-15, 1924.	Week Mar. 3-8, 1924.	Week Mar. 12-17, 1923.	Week Mar. 10-15, 1924.	Week Mar. 3-8, 1924.	Week Mar. 12-17, 1923.
1,001 lbs. up.....	324	94	106	8.7	2.8	4.5	1,051	1,095	1,094	$8.27	$8.47	7.89
901–1,000 lbs....	547	454	203	14.6	13.7	8.5	955	949	948	7.55	7.64	7.60
801–900 lbs......	961	654	580	25.2	19.7	24.4	859	843	849	7.37	6.92	7.48
701–800 lbs......	621	830	519	16.0	25.0	21.8	742	750	739	7.03	6.70	7.46
700 lbs. down....	1,287	1,288	972	33.9	38.8	40.8	586	602	608	6.26	6.39	6.57
Total..........	3,740	3,320	2,380	100.0	100.0	100.0	775	748	748	7.18	6.89	7.27

Meat Prices Respond to Smaller Supplies.

Boston, New York, Philadelphia, and Chicago.

The outstanding feature in the wholesale fresh-meat trade at eastern markets and Chicago during the week ended March 14, consisted in a marked reduction in supplies and a fair response in the form of price advances. With the single exception of mutton, receipts of western dressed meats at eastern markets were considerably lighter than a week earlier, and at Chicago supplies were barely normal. Consumptive demand did not seem materially greater and was uneven but lighter offerings placed sellers in a position to hold and in most instances to advance prices somewhat.

Beef.—Receipts of beef at eastern markets were smaller than during the preceding week. Medium and good grades predominated in both steer and cow beef offerings, choice and common steers and common cows being comparatively scarce, but this situation seemed satisfactory to both buyers and sellers, although efforts were made to keep supplies in line with the demand. The cow beef market closely paralleled that of steers.

At Chicago beef supplies showed some decrease as compared with the preceding week, but were fully ample for the slow demand. Higher dressed costs forced prices upward 50¢–$1 and the market in general held steady at the advance.

The light supplies of bull beef were confined largely to New York and Chicago, prices holding about steady.

Kosher chucks and plates advanced around $2 during the week at New York, due to a rather limited supply while hinds and ribs were slow with average reductions of around $1. At other markets prices were mostly unchanged.

Veal.—Receipts of veal were only moderate and while at New York prices at the close were unevenly $1–$3 higher than a week earlier, distinct evidences of weakness were apparent at times. On the other hand, prices at Philadelphia declined around $1 for the week. Other markets were generally steady throughout the period.

Lamb.—Receipts of lamb were generally light at eastern markets, with strictly choice kinds relatively scarce. Trading was moderately active and the trend of prices upward, advances of $3–$4 being made at New York with some sales up to $30, while Philadelphia advanced $2–$3 and Boston $1. Heavy-weight kinds were in the majority, a seasonal characteristic. At Chicago, prices in the moderate offerings were moved upward around $1 at the opening of the week and held steady thereafter, although attempts were made to obtain further advances.

Mutton.—The supply of mutton was very light at Boston and Philadelphia, but receipts at New York showed a substantial increase. Despite the increased offerings at that market, trade was brisk and prices were fully $1 higher for the week, which was also true at Philadelphia. In some instances new price records for the season were established, a few choice light weight carcasses selling up to $22.50 at New York. At Chicago the light offerings scored a full dollar advance.

Pork.—Supplies were moderate at eastern markets and demand far from brisk. Despite this fact sellers were able to maintain firm prices and in some instances to advance them 50¢–$1 for the week. Toward the close, however, some weakness was apparent due to a slackening in demand. Heavy loins continued scarce. At Chicago the fairly liberal supplies were moved early in the week at prices strong to $1 higher than on the preceding Friday, with a further advance of $1 at midweek. However, the higher prices attracted heavy shipments from other packing centers and an uneven weakness developed.

Chicago Wholesale Prices of Cured Pork and Pork Products.[1]

Week of March 10–15, 1924, with Comparisons.

[In dollars per 100 pounds.]

Commodity.	Mar. 10–15, 1924.	Mar. 3–8, 1924.	Mar. 12–17, 1923.	3-year average.[2]
Hams No. 1, smoked, 14–16 lbs. average.	21.25	21.25	21.50	27.13
Hams No. 2, smoked, 14–16 lbs. average.	19.25	19.75	19.00	24.42
Picnics, smoked, 4–8 lbs. average.	11.62	11.75	12.00	15.67
Bacon No. 1, 6–8 lbs. average.	24.25	24.75	30.00	35.33
Bacon No. 2, 6–8 lbs. average.	18.25	16.50	21.75	26.75
Bellies, dry salt, 14–16 lbs. average.	12.88	11.75	14.25	16.00
Backs, dry salt, 14–16 lbs. average.	12.00	11.00	11.75	13.04
Pure lard, tierces.	12.62	13.25	14.00	14.00
Compound lard, tierces.	13.00	13.50	13.75	12.92

[1] Based on average prices to retailers.
[2] Based on average prices for the following weeks: Mar. 14–19, 1921; Mar. 13–18, 1922; and Mar. 12–17, 1923.

Average Wholesale Prices of Western Dressed Fresh Meats.

Week of March 10–15, 1924, with Comparisons.

[In dollars per 100 pounds.]

Kind and grade.	Chicago.				New York.			
	Mar. 10–15, 1924.	Mar. 3–8, 1924.	Mar. 12–17, 1923.	Three-year average.[2]	Mar. 10–15, 1924.	Mar. 3–8, 1924.	Mar. 12–17, 1923.	Three-year average.[1]
Beef and Veal.								
Beef:								
Steer—								
Choice	18.50	18.50	16.50	16.90	17.20	17.10	14.50	[1]14.25
Good	16.50	16.35	15.25	15.52	15.20	15.00	13.50	14.97
Medium	14.25	14.20	13.35	13.75	13.65	13.20	12.00	13.90
Common	12.00	12.10	10.75	11.53	12.55	12.00	10.50	12.85
Cow—								
Good	11.75	11.70	10.75	11.85	11.60	11.90	10.50	12.23
Medium	10.50	10.30	9.50	10.52	10.85	11.05	9.50	11.20
Common	8.50	8.45	8.50	9.52	9.80	10.15	8.75	10.50
Bull—								
Medium					9.75	9.75	8.50	9.68
Common	8.25	8.26	7.62	8.43	8.75	8.75	7.75	9.02
Veal:								
Choice	18.50	18.50	17.50	17.93	18.80	18.90	17.10	19.57
Good	16.50	16.50	15.50	16.60	16.60	16.80	16.00	17.33
Medium	14.00	14.00	14.50	15.02	13.30	13.50	14.70	15.53
Common	11.00	11.00	11.50	12.17	10.50	10.40	11.50	12.70
Fresh Pork Cuts.								
Hams:								
12–16 lbs. average	15.50	15.25	17.50	22.17	17.00	17.50	17.00	22.67
Loins:								
8–10 lbs. average	16.85	13.50	15.00	20.27	14.40	14.40	15.30	19.73
10–12 lbs. average	15.75	12.80	13.95	19.18	13.70	13.65	14.30	18.43
12–14 lbs. average	14.25	11.90	13.25	18.02	13.00	12.65	13.45	17.37
14–16 lbs. average	13.25	11.35	12.55	16.75	12.50	12.29	12.70	16.38
16 lbs. and over	12.30	10.70	11.50	15.30	11.55	11.30	11.50	15.23
Shoulders:								
Skinned	10.20	9.40	11.60	14.03	10.50	10.40	12.80	14.93
Picnics—								
4–6 lbs. average	8.95	8.55	9.95	12.80	9.50	9.65	10.50	
6–8 lbs. average	8.55	8.25	9.45	12.07	8.75	8.50	9.50	13.03
Butts:								
Boston style	12.30	11.35	12.60	15.83	13.10	13.50	13.75	16.67
Spare ribs	9.85	8.15	9.45	11.32	9.00	9.00	11.50	13.00
Lamb and Mutton.								
Lamb:								
Choice	27.50	26.50	24.10	24.87	28.10	26.80	24.50	25.73
Good	25.90	25.10	21.00	22.67	26.40	25.30	23.50	24.50
Medium	24.50	23.90	18.00	20.50	24.90	23.60	22.50	22.60
Common	22.00	20.80	15.50	18.00			20.50	[2]22.05
Mutton:								
Good	18.50	17.50	12.50	14.67	19.90	19.50	13.50	15.12
Medium	16.50	15.50	11.00	12.67	18.40	18.00	12.25	13.45
Common	13.00	12.50	8.50	10.17	16.20	16.00	10.50	12.05

[1] Based on average prices for the following weeks: Mar. 14–19, 1921; Mar. 13–18, 1922; and Mar. 12–17, 1923.
[2] Two-year average.

Boston Wool Market Quotations.

Prices in general were firm on the Boston wool market during the week ended March 17.

Trading has been quiet but well distributed, with no particular demand for any special lines, although a little more inquiry was being made for the finer grades. A feature of the situation from a supply standpoint was the reexportation of approximately 150,000 pounds of foreign wools held in bond which were cleared for export during the week ended March 8.

Class and grade.	Grease basis.[1]	Scoured basis.	
	Fleece.	Fleece.	Territory.
	Per pound.	*Per pound.*	*Per pound.*
Fine strictly combing	$0.57	$1.40–1.45	$1.40–1.45
Fine French combing	.51–0.52	1.28–1.30	1.30–1.35
Fine clothing	.49–.50	1.22–1.25	1.22–1.25
½ blood strictly combing	.57	1.30–1.32	1.32–1.35
½ blood French combing	.50–.51	1.20–1.25	1.25–1.30
½ blood clothing	.50–.51	1.18–1.20	1.18–1.22
⅜ blood strictly clothing	.57	1.12–1.15	1.15–1.15
⅜ blood clothing	.49–.50	1.00–1.02	1.02–1.05
¼ blood strictly clothing	.54–.55	.93–.98	.98–1.02
¼ blood clothing	.44–.46	.83–.88	.85–.90
Low ¼ blood strictly clothing	.47–.49	.78–.82	.82–.85
Common and braid	.43	.65–.68	.65–.68

[1] Average quotations on the better class of fleece wools similar to Ohio and Pennsylvania. The better class of Michigan, New York, Wisconsin, and Missouri wool 1 to 2¢ less. Kentucky and similar wool 2 to 5¢ higher, depending on the particular lots offered. The above quotations depend to some extent on the individual lots.

Averages Prices of Live Stock, Week of March 10–15, 1924, with Comparisons.

[In dollars per 100 pounds.]

Kind and grade.	Chicago. Mar. 10-15, 1924.	Mar. 3-8, 1924.	Mar. 12-17, 1923.	3-year aver-age.[2]	East St. Louis. Mar. 10-15, 1924.	Mar. 3-8, 1924.	Mar. 12-17, 1923.	3-year aver-age.[2]	Fort Worth.[1] Mar. 10-15, 1924.	Mar. 3-8, 1924.	Kansas City. Mar. 10-15, 1924.	Mar. 3-8, 1924.	Mar. 12-17, 1923.	3-year aver-age.[2]	Omaha. Mar. 10-15, 1924.	Mar. 3-8, 1924.	Mar. 12-17, 1923.	3-year aver-age.[2]	South St. Paul. Mar. 10-15, 1924.	Mar. 3-8, 1924.	Mar. 12-17, 1923.	3-year aver-age.[2]
Cattle.																						
Slaughter cattle and calves:																						
Steers (1,100 lbs. up)--																						
Choice and prime..	11.84	11.80	10.22	9.91	11.62	11.52	10.28	9.63			11.00	10.99	9.92	9.41	11.10	11.11	9.75	9.27	10.75	10.75		8.55[10]
Good..	10.70	10.78	9.57	9.25	10.65	10.60	9.57	8.96	7.25	7.25	9.82	9.62	8.64	8.64	10.00	9.98	8.85	8.53	9.42	9.30		
Medium..	9.03	9.28	8.73	8.47	9.02	8.98	8.52	8.15	7.25	7.25	8.42	8.10	7.92	7.82	8.46	8.00	7.82	7.65	7.92	8.00	7.65	7.69
Common..	7.35	7.54	7.46	7.54	7.38	7.26	7.20	7.21	5.38	5.38	6.62	6.10	7.06	7.17	6.86	6.70	6.75	7.00	6.12	6.12	6.62	6.81
Steers(1,100 lbs.down)—																						
Choice and prime..	11.75	11.69	10.28	9.92	11.62	11.55	10.28	9.59			11.00	10.99	9.78	9.26	10.98	11.06	9.75	9.27	10.75	10.75		
Good..	10.57	10.70	9.59	9.23	10.62	10.58	9.44	8.84	8.25	8.25	9.62	9.58	8.76	8.43	9.86	9.96	8.88	8.45	9.42	9.30		8.54[10]
Medium..	8.89	9.14	8.64	8.38	9.02	8.96	8.33	8.01	6.88	6.88	8.12	8.10	7.86	7.70	8.42	8.32	7.88	7.65	7.80	7.88	7.65	7.69
Common..	6.80	7.00	7.26	7.32	6.88	6.78	6.96	6.93	5.12	5.15	6.32	6.10	6.73	6.88	6.54	6.33	6.50	6.77	5.88	5.88	6.50	6.67
Canner and cutter.	4.82	4.70	4.50	4.47	4.50	4.40	4.00	3.93	3.25	3.26	4.30	4.00	3.75	3.71	4.34	4.20	3.88	4.09	3.75	3.75	3.52	3.67
Light yearling steers and heifers-																						
Good and prime (800 lbs. down)[3].	10.80	10.90			10.22	10.13					8.50	8.50	9.62	9.62	9.84	9.74			9.75	9.75		
Heifers—																						
Good and choice (850 lbs. up)	9.04	9.04	[4]7.70	7.17	8.08	7.88	[4]7.36	7.16	7.00	6.90	8.00	7.95	6.48	6.42	8.38	8.28	[4]6.75	6.54	8.12	8.05	[4]6.45	6.38
Common and medium (all weights)..	6.40	6.42			5.18	5.00			4.62	4.42	5.06	4.82			5.75	5.62			5.12	5.05		
Cows—																						
Good and choice..	6.67	6.66	[6]6.10	6.00	6.80	6.22	5.95	5.83	5.50	5.25	6.20	5.90	[5]5.44	5.19	6.24	6.10	[5]5.55	5.69	6.00	5.92	[5]5.30	5.33
Common and medium..	4.96	4.94			4.98	4.62			4.32	4.12	4.32	4.12			4.56	4.41			4.25	4.18		
Canner and cutter.	3.40	3.35	3.78	3.74	3.30	3.06	3.52	3.70	2.42	2.52	3.00	2.98	3.36	3.49	3.10	3.02	3.58	3.66	2.75	2.75	3.15	3.10
Bulls—																						
Good and choice (beef yearlings excluded)[3]..	5.80	5.83			5.75	5.75			4.25	4.25	5.38	5.38			5.36	5.40			4.88	4.88		
Common to medium (canner and bologna)[3]	4.54	4.46			4.12	4.05			2.88	2.88	3.88	3.85			4.06	4.08			3.88	3.88		
Calves—																						
Medium to choice (100 lbs. down)..	9.85	9.82	[9]9.28	9.41	9.28	8.65	[8]8.35	8.77	7.38	7.38	8.30	8.50	[8]8.20	8.34	8.62	8.62	[8]8.80	8.70	7.40	7.18	[8]6.48	6.86
Medium to choice (190-260 lbs.)..	8.80	8.68			8.65	8.05			7.12	7.12	7.05	7.28			7.80	7.80			5.75	5.75		
Medium to choice (260 lbs. up)..	6.95	6.95	[6]6.15	6.08	6.40	6.45	[6]6.75	6.58	6.75	6.75	6.26	6.22	[6]6.02	5.87	6.52	6.22	[6]6.00	6.38	4.75	4.75	[6]5.50	5.17
Cull and common (100 lbs. down)[3]..	6.40	6.52			5.25	5.35			4.25	4.25	5.00	5.00			5.68	5.62			4.40	4.50		
Cull and common (190 lbs. up)[3]..	5.78	5.89			4.00	4.00			4.00	4.00	4.12	4.10			4.58	4.50			3.25	3.25		
Feeder and stocker cattle and calves:																						
Steers, common to choice (750 lbs. up)[1]..	7.20	7.19	7.86	7.52	6.38	6.30	6.94	7.16	5.85	5.60	6.85	6.75	7.40	7.44	7.01	6.90	6.90	7.24	5.75	5.70	6.12	6.46
Steers, common to choice(750 lbs.down)[1]	6.58	6.62	6.36	6.70	6.00	6.00	6.00	[10]6.02	5.60	5.35	6.25	6.25	6.84	6.77	6.53	6.50	6.21	6.61	5.50	5.35	5.62	5.97
Steers, inferior (all weights)[3]..	4.32	4.30			4.00	3.92			3.25	3.18	3.75	3.75			4.03	3.99			3.00	3.00		
Cows and heifers, common-choice)..	4.45	4.34	4.65	4.98	4.12	4.05	4.75	5.39	3.00	3.00	4.12	4.10	4.54	4.97	4.18	4.38	4.96	5.32	3.62	3.92	4.00	4.25
Calves, common-choice[4]									5.25	5.18	5.88	5.85	0.38	6.11	5.88	5.75	6.19	6.37	4.88	4.88		
Hogs.																						
Top (highest price, not average)..	7.65	7.70	8.85	11.50	7.75	7.65	8.75	11.40	7.45	7.60	7.40	7.35	8.40	10.90	7.30	7.30	8.25	10.75	7.15	7.15	8.30	10.75
Bulk of sales..	7.36	7.36	8.23	9.50	7.43	7.40	8.48	9.73	7.05	7.14	7.11	7.03	7.99	9.66	6.95	6.98	7.99	9.04	6.95	6.98	7.98	9.09
Heavy weight (250-350 lbs.) medium-choice..	7.43	7.45	8.19	9.31	7.43	7.43	8.36	9.38	7.00	7.00	7.20	7.20	8.05	9.00	7.10	7.11	7.99	8.97	6.98	7.00	7.88	8.86
Medium weight (200-250 lbs.) medium-choice..	7.38	7.40	8.37	9.63	7.46	7.45	8.45	9.73	7.10	7.14	7.08	7.05	8.11	9.19	6.98	6.94	8.00	9.13	6.97	6.98	7.98	9.10
Light weight (160-200 lbs.) common-choice..	7.18	7.24	8.58	9.68	7.20	7.14	8.50	9.87	6.52	6.57	6.72	6.68	8.08	9.22	6.70	6.64	7.92	9.20	6.88	6.91	8.07	9.92
Light lights (130-160 lbs.) common-choice..	6.68	6.69	8.32	9.73	6.78	6.66	8.34	9.68	5.99	6.05	6.05	6.01	7.95	9.18	6.28	6.13			6.47	6.60	7.91	[10]8.90
Packing hogs:																						
Smooth..	6.65	6.62	7.50	8.53	6.50	6.38	7.41	8.19	6.36	6.31	6.35	6.30	7.33	8.05	6.47	6.57	7.39	8.27	6.71	6.35	6.88	8.03
Rough..	6.40	6.38	7.25	8.17	6.30	6.12	7.27	7.90	5.88	5.79	6.18	6.15	7.20	7.69	6.30	6.37	7.20	7.88	5.99	5.93	6.62	7.69
Slaughter pigs (130 lbs. down) medium-choice....	5.31	5.29	7.71	9.03	6.02	5.88	7.10	8.72	4.56	4.88	5.73	5.63							5.80	5.83	7.71	9.40
Feeder and stocker pigs (70-130 lbs. down) common-choice..					5.20	4.97	6.50	8.14			4.98	4.82	7.10	8.82	4.77	4.75	6.75	8.74	4.88	4.94	7.73	9.47
Sheep and lambs.																						
Slaughter sheep and lambs:																						
Lambs-																						
Light and handy wt. (84 lbs. down) medium-prime..	15.14	15.16	14.08	12.73	15.02	14.88	13.88	12.73	14.25		14.68	14.54	13.54	12.28	14.74	14.52	13.62	12.38	14.32	14.32	13.46	12.01
All weights, cull and common..	12.50	12.55	11.40	10.23	12.42	12.12	11.25	9.89	11.25		11.50	11.70	11.12	9.73	11.88	11.72	11.15	9.86	11.58	11.65	10.62	9.26
Yearling wethers, medium-prime..	12.78	12.80	11.62	10.70	12.50	12.40	11.25	10.16			12.05	11.75	11.05	9.98	12.25	11.95	11.28	10.14	12.05	11.80	10.88	9.91
Wethers (2 yrs. old and over) medium-prime..	9.88	9.75	9.25	8.60	9.92	9.50	8.62	8.62	8.70	8.40	9.28	9.38	8.38	7.62	9.54	9.29	8.38	7.76	8.95	8.75	8.00	7.39
Ewes, common-choice[3]..	8.86	8.50			8.48	8.25			7.50	7.05	8.12	8.12			8.42	8.10			7.96	7.72		
Ewes, canner and cull[3].	4.95	4.75			4.50	4.50			4.00	3.70	4.38	4.38			4.50	4.25			4.50	4.12		
Feeding sheep and lambs:																						
Feeding lambs, medium-choice..	14.63	14.45	14.26	11.72							13.38	11.02	14.50	14.08	13.75	11.56						

Note: Classification of Livestock changed July 2, 1923.
[1] Fort Worth began reporting Jan. 15, 1923.
[2] Based on average prices for the following weeks: Mar. 14–19, 1921; Mar. 13–18, 1922; Mar. 12–17, 1923.
[3] No comparable grade in former classification.
[4] Old classification combined common to choice; comparable figures are on that description.
[5] In old classification classed as light and medium weight.
[6] In old classification classed as heavy weight.
[7] Data previous to July, 1923, are averages of feeder steers, 1,000 and 750–1,000 lbs. in former classification.
[8] In old classification classed as stocker steers, common-choice.
[9] Data previous to July, 1923, are averages of stocker calves, good and choice and common and medium in former classification.
[10] Two-year average.

Stocker and Feeder Shipments.

Week March 8-14, 1924, with Comparisons.

Origin and destination.	Cattle and calves.		Hogs.		Sheep.	
	Week Mar. 8-14, 1924.	Per cent of average of corresponding week 1920, 1921, 1922, 1923.	Week Mar. 8-14, 1924.	Per cent of average of corresponding week 1920, 1921, 1922, 1923.	Week Mar. 8-14, 1924.	Per cent of average of corresponding week 1920, 1921, 1922, 1923.
Market origin:						
Chicago	4,171	74.8			6,022	155.4
Denver	3,884	167.6	1,827		2,797	112.0
East St. Louis	806	33.9	376	19.5		
Fort Worth	1,614	50.3	108	5.8	177	22.2
Indianapolis	318	62.6	67	28.3		
Kansas City	9,908	89.4	3,844	32.6	2,177	90.3
Oklahoma City	1,511	76.0	152	20.6		
Omaha	7,032	103.1	414	313.6	3,067	125.3
St. Joseph	1,390	127.3	41	23.2	2,575	243.2
St. Paul	2,610	52.1	91	2.8	2,929	
Sioux City	3,158	71.3	65	14.7		
Wichita	2,799	101.3	674	242.4		
Total	39,146	84.1	7,359	32.8	19,744	151.6
State destination:						
California	1,162		1,164			
Colorado	1,284	170.9	223	185.8		
Connecticut	28					
Illinois	3,956	75.8	711	28.9	1,394	133.0
Indiana	1,284	87.3	97	21.3		
Iowa	7,092	73.3	1,854	39.0	2,029	299.7
Kansas	7,044	91.8	513	68.2	797	82.2
Kentucky	20	4.5				
Louisiana	139					
Massachusetts			181			
Michigan	350	74.2			6,134	341.3
Minnesota	527	45.6	89	13.6	310	66.5
Missouri	4,047	89.4	1,252	45.2	2,885	138.0
Nebraska	7,556	115.0	730	130.8	4,606	179.7
North Dakota	43	238.9				
Ohio	729	56.5				
Oklahoma	1,820	80.5				
Pennsylvania	31	17.1			150	80.2
South Dakota	309	89.4				
Tennessee	30	90.9				
Texas	983	38.8	435	161.7	418	52.1
Utah	131					
Virginia	62	23.0				
Wisconsin	554	65.5			1,021	287.6
Wyoming	25	119.0	140			
Total	39,146	84.1	7,359	32.8	19,744	151.6

Season Comparisons of Stocker and Feeder Shipments.

	Cattle and calves.	Hogs.	Sheep.
July 1, 1923, to Mar. 14, 1924	3,191,572	451,043	3,213,877
Same period one year ago	3,443,572	413,439	2,804,014
Same period two years ago	2,402,389	216,788	2,209,258
Same period three years ago	2,266,028	274,495	2,502,134
Current period as per cent of average of three previous periods	117.2	149.6	128.3

Beef Steers Sold Out of First Hands for Slaughter at Chicago.

Week March 10-15, 1924, with Comparisons.

Grade.	Number of head.			Per cent of total by grades.			Average weight (pounds).			Average price per 100 pounds.		
	Week Mar. 15, 1924.	Week Mar. 8-, 1924.	Week Mar. 17, 1923.	Week Mar. 15, 1924.	Week Mar. 8-, 1924.	Week Mar. 17, 1923.	Week Mar. 15, 1924.	Week Mar. 8-, 1924.	Week Mar. 17, 1923.	Week Mar. 15, 1924.	Week Mar. 8-, 1924.	Week Mar. 17, 1923.
Choice and prime	491	940	797	2.2	4.1	3.1	1,323	1,418	1,320	$11.70	$11.54	$9.94
Good	4,077	3,591	4,956	18.3	15.6	19.2	1,254	1,253	1,231	10.28	10.47	9.48
Medium	13,787	13,108	16,357	61.8	57.1	63.5	1,079	1,086	1,101	8.80	9.11	8.69
Common	3,951	5,328	3,651	17.7	23.2	14.2	837	873	935	7.30	7.58	7.61
Total	22,306	22,967	25,761	100.0	100.0	100.0	1,073	1,077	1,108	8.99	9.19	8.78

For "Wool Imports at Three Ports" see page 192.

91020°—24——2

Fruits and Vegetables

Apple Exports Still Large.

Apple supplies continued heavy, with markets generally dull. Higher prices at Idaho shipping points were about the only bright feature of the potato situation; general price trend was downward. Northern cabbage lost another $10 per ton in jobbing centers, but southern celery and lettuce advanced during the week ending March 15. Florida tomato supplies were increasing, while strawberries almost disappeared from the market. The net decrease of 1,250 cars in the week's output of 16 fruits and vegetables was caused chiefly by smaller movement of potatoes and cabbage. Total shipments were 13,240 cars.

Apples.—Although recent exports of apples have not been so heavy as previously, there still is a good movement to the United Kingdom and other countries. Reports of the International Apple Shippers' Association to March 8 indicate total exports, including about one-third Canadian stock, of 2,840,000 barrels and 4,514,000 boxes, compared with 1,581,000 barrels and 2,990,000 boxes to the same time last season. This is a total increase of two-thirds. During March and April, 1923, about 125,000 barrels and 400,000 boxes of apples were shipped abroad and the end-of-the-season movement this year probably will not be less.

EASTERN APPLES PROMINENT.

New York State has become the leading source of current supply. Shipments from the Northwest have decreased sharply, and Washington is shipping 200 cars per week less than New York. Much of New York's output is small-size stock for export trade. Large blocks of A2½-inch Baldwins recently sold at shipping points for $3.50-$3.60 per barrel, with A2½-inch stock bringing $3-$3.15. One car of Rhode Island Greenings brought $4.25, but later sales were made at $4. Orchard-run apples, as they lay in storage, have been closed out by some growers at $1.75-$2.10 per barrel.

Heavy arrivals were reported in New York City, some, of course, to be exported. During the second week of March about 375 cars of barreled stock and 240 cars of western apples were received, and the market was dull except for best stock. Eastern Baldwins ranged $3.50-$4 in New York, and slightly higher in other cities. Most desirable lots of York Imperials ranged up to $4.50 with Greenings and Staymar Winesaps touching $5. In Kansas City, best midwestern Jonathans were jobbing at $6 per barrel.

Northwestern Extra Fancy Winesaps, medium to large sizes, were steady at $2.25-$2.50 per box on the Chicago market, and strengthened to $1.55 f. o. b. Yakima, Wash. This variety ranged irregularly in the East, bringing $2.15-$2.75 in New York. Top price on Delicious was $3.50.

Total cold-storage holdings on March 1 were 2,747,000 barrels, 8,832,000 boxes, and 825,000 bushel baskets. This is 36% more barreled apples than the year before, and about 90% above the five-year average. Boxed holdings represent an increase of 58% over last March and 80% over the five-year average. Aggregate stocks were nearly half again as large as on March 1, 1923, and about 88% above average. Many apples long in cold storage show scald and other defects.

CABBAGE MARKETS WEAKER.

New York Danish-type *cabbage* declined further to the wide range of $33-$60 per ton in city markets. Poorer quality is becoming evident. The few sales of Northern Danish brought $40-$60. New York and Wisconsin shipments decreased 50% to 95 cars and 16 cars, respectively. New cabbage came at the rate of 100 cars per day, compared with 30 a year ago. Demand for Florida stock in 1½-bushel hampers was somewhat draggy at $1.25-$2.25. Texas flat type ranged $50-$60 per ton in the Middle West and $60-$80 in the East. Movement from the 575 acres in the Eagle Lake-Wharton section of Texas is expected to start by April 1.

Potatoes.—With a daily average of 260 cars on track, the Chicago potato market sagged to a closing range of $1.10-$1.25 per 100 pounds for sacked Northern round whites. Bulk stock declined to $1.20-$1.30. North Central shipping points also weakened. Eastern round whites, however, ruled generally $1.65-$1.90 in leading cities. In Idaho the cash track price for sacked Rurals advanced to high mark of 90¢, and best Russets for California shipment brought $1.60. Chicago sales of Russets reached $2.60. Total shipments decreased about 435 cars to a weekly volume of 5,000. Acreage around Eagle Lake, Tex., is estimated to be 4,500, only half of last year's plantings.

Celery markets closed firm to stronger, Florida Golden Self-Blanching ranging $3.50–$3.75 per crate in most cities, and advancing to $2.75 f. o. b. shipping points, where demand exceeded the available supply. Average yield in Florida this season has been about two cars per acre. A few sales of California Golden Heart, mostly in the West, were made at $5.50–$6.50 per crate. Movement from California increased about 30 cars, but Florida's output was 160 cars less.

LETTUCE PRICES HIGHER.

Imperial Valley *lettuce* shipments decreased by over 100 cars. Movement from Florida also was less, and there was a loss of 140 cars in the week's total output from all sections. With arrivals much lighter in city markets, California Iceberg type advanced to a range of $4–$4.50 per crate. In New York the advance was $1.50. Florida lettuce also gained sharply in that city, ranging $4.50–$5 per 1½-bushel hamper. At El Centro, Calif., the f. o. b. price advanced $1.50–$1.85, reaching a top of $3–$3.50 per crate.

Tomatoes.—Florida tomatoes sold firm at $3.50–$4.25 in New York City. Quality of East Coast stock has improved lately, and there are prospects of a good crop in the Lake Okeechobee section, with first cars expected by April 5. Cold weather has delayed the tomatoes farther north. Total plantings in Florida are estimated about 48,000 acres, compared with 36,360 last season. Early reports indicate that Texas may have 950 acres of tomatoes for spring shipment in Dimmit County and 200 acres near Crystal City.

MISCELLANEOUS PRODUCTS.

Texas *spinach* advanced 5¢ at Austin, bringing 65¢ per bushel, and demand exceeded supply. At Laredo the price remained mostly around 60¢. Texas stock advanced to a range of $1.25–$1.50 in city markets. Weekly shipments of California *asparagus* increased from 10 to 47 cars. In leading cities California stock sold at $8–$10 per standard crate. About this time last season prices ranged from $15 to $20, followed by sharp declines. *Cauliflower* from California strengthened to $2–$3 per pony crate, with shipments from California and Oregon almost 100 cars less. Florida *peppers* maintained a range of $5.50–$6.50 per crate in most cities, going as low as $4.50 in New York. Some fair-quality *strawberries* appeared on the market. Best stock ranged from 50¢ per quart in Kansas City to 75¢–85¢ in Philadelphia. Florida's output dropped from 27 to 11 cars.

Carload Shipments of Fruits and Vegetables.

Week of March 9–15 and season to March 15, with Comparisons.

Product.	Mar. 9–15, 1924.	Mar. 2–8, 1924.	Mar. 11–17, 1923.	Total this season to Mar. 15.	Total last season to Mar. 17.	Total last season.
Apples:						
Western States	621	713	879	59,742	44,028	46,286
Eastern States	832	796	689	62,500	61,532	65,997
Asparagus	47	10	(1)	60	(1)	773
Cabbage:						
Old crop	147	273	277	36,113	41,196	41,327
New crop	696	817	189	4,644	[2] 1,645	[2] 36,113
Cauliflower	219	310	225	3,666	4,008	4,616
Celery:						
Old crop	141	109	38	16,624	14,729	14,921
New crop (Florida)	388	549	479	4,043	[2] 3,308	[2] 6,398
Grapefruit	597	651	(1)	13,158	(1)	17,684
Lemons	201	224	(1)	3,654	(1)	8,194
Lettuce	531	672	928	13,115	11,453	27,689
Onions	432	451	328	26,807	28,800	29,753
Oranges	2,188	2,003	(1)	38,032	(1)	67,961
Potatoes:						
Sweet	127	162	376	13,883	19,001	21,569
White—						
1923 crop	5,015	5,449	5,183	195,006	204,922	254,158
1924 crop	12	5	7	19	7	3,493
Spinach	[2] 202	237	419	4,312	4,251	7,354
Strawberries	11	27	92	442	860	17,896
Tomatoes	350	462	534	2,757	2,199	24,024
Vegetables, mixed	425	568	478	4,833	4,084	23,951
Total	13,242	14,488	10,821	503,010	441,065	677,501

[1] Unavailable.
[2] Not included in totals.

Arrivals and Prices of Fruits and Vegetables.

Arrivals Include All Varieties of Each Product for the Week March 11–17, 1924, with Comparisons; Prices are for March 17, 1924, with Comparisons, and are for the Variety or Varieties Specified.

POTATOES (Prices quoted on Eastern and Northern Round Whites, sacked per 100 pounds).

Markets.	Mar. 11–17, 1924.	Mar. 4–10, 1924.	Mar. 13–19, 1923.	Jan. 1–Mar. 17, 1924.	Jan. 1–Mar. 19, 1923.	Mar. 17, 1924	Mar. 10, 1924.	Mar. 10, 1923.
		Total car-lot arrivals.					Jobbing range.	
New York	323	455	472	3,870	3,504	$1.65–1.85	$1.65–1.85	$1.65–1.85
Boston	265	288	179	3,208	2,074	1.90–2.00	1.90–2.00	1.90–2.00
Philadelphia	164	200	135	1,538	1,053	1.50–1.75	1.65–1.90	1.75
Baltimore	32	47	26	366	181	1.65–1.75	1.65–1.75	1.65–1.75
Pittsburgh	157	148	155	1,238	1,107	1.65–1.85	1.75–1.85	1.60–1.65
Cincinnati	98	68	113	645	556	1.50–1.55	1.35–1.55	1.35–1.45
Chicago	435	268	308	3,555	3,525	1.10–1.25	1.25–1.50	1.05–1.15
St. Louis	91	114	130	784	906	1.65	1.60	[2] 1.45
Kansas City	339	421	351	2,482	1,969	[1] 1.35–1.40	[1] 1.40–1.50	[1] 1.25

APPLES (Prices quoted on Eastern Baldwins, barrels).

New York	377	301	171	2,680	1,810	$3.50–4.00	$3.75–4.00	$5.00–5.25
Boston	10	15	10	127	136	4.50–6.00	4.50–5.25	6.00–6.50
Philadelphia	30	36	24	426	366	3.75–4.00	4.00–5.25	5.50–5.75
Baltimore	13	15	11	178	131	3.75–4.00	3.50	5.25–5.50
Pittsburgh	71	79	81	772	829	3.50–4.00	4.00–4.50	5.00–5.50
Cincinnati	21	29	21	302	211	4.25–4.75	4.00–4.50	5.25–5.50
Chicago	34	29	30	262	290	4.50–5.00	4.50–5.00	5.25–5.50
St. Louis		2	1	27	124	4.50	4.50–5.00	
Kansas City	11	2	2	35	28	[4] 5.00–5.50	[4] 5.00–5.50	[4] 5.50

APPLES (Prices quoted on Northwestern Extra Fancy Winesaps, boxes).

New York	239	264	158	2,418	1,625	$2.15–2.75	$2.40–2.75	$2.25–2.75
Philadelphia	45	45	73	410	444	2.00–2.50		2.40–2.75
Baltimore	10	9	21	136	206	[5] 2.25	2.10–2.25	2.50–3.00
Pittsburgh	51	42	65	496	449	2.00–2.10	2.00–2.25	2.25–2.50
Chicago	73	77	120	682	2,077	2.25–2.50	2.25–2.50	2.50–2.60
Kansas City	24	30	18	302	342	2.40	2.40	2.50

ONIONS (Prices quoted on Eastern and Middlewestern Yellow Varieties, sacked per 100 pounds).

New York	171	185	126	1,759	1,444	$2.00–2.50	$2.00–2.50	$4.25–4.50
Boston	22	31	11	208	341	2.25–2.50	2.00–2.50	2.75–3.00
Philadelphia	48	38	33	497	395	2.25–2.35	2.50–2.65	3.25–3.50
Baltimore	13	13	5	132	117	2.25–2.50	2.50	3.50–3.75
Pittsburgh	39	28	35	317	266	2.00–2.25	2.00–2.25	3.50–3.75
Cincinnati	15	7	10	113	69	2.00–2.25	1.75–2.25	3.75–4.00
Chicago	17	27	68	314	401	2.25–2.50	2.00–2.25	2.50–2.60
St. Louis	15	12	14	175	170	[3] 3.00	[3] 3.00	[3] 2.15
Kansas City	13	12	14	159	180	[3] 3.00–3.25	[3] 3.00–3.25	[3] 2.00–2.25

CABBAGE (Prices quoted on New York Danish Type, bulk per ton).

New York	176	110	84	1,124	774	$33.00–46.00	$45.00–55.00	$55.00–60.00
Boston	30	37	27	288	264	[7] [8] 3.50		
Philadelphia	87	91	57	671	531	50.00	45.00–50.00	35.00–45.00
Baltimore	47	41	28	287	283	40.00–55.00	50.00–60.00	50.00–60.00
Pittsburgh	62	56	39	438	325	45.00–50.00	50.00–55.00	50.00–60.00
Cincinnati	28	30	16	204	138	50.00–60.00	70.00–75.00	57.00–65.00
Chicago	115	79	69	840	629	[7] [8] 3.15–3.25	[7] [8] 3.25–3.35	[8] 4.50
St. Louis	52	76	47	464	355	[8] 55.00–60.00	[8] 50.00–55.00	[8] 87.50
Kansas City	13	26	12	226	191	[8] 55.00	[8] 60.00	[8] [4] 50

SWEET POTATOES (Prices quoted on Delaware and Maryland Yellow Varieties, bushel hampers).

New York	30	32	27	450	569	$3.50–3.75	$3.50–3.75	$0.65–0.90
Boston	6	5	15	52	138	3.50	3.50–3.75	.85–1.00
Philadelphia	7	5	9	129	91	3.25	3.25–3.50	.60
Baltimore	8	9	5	65	93	3.25	3.00–3.25	.50–.65
Pittsburgh	19	11	30	244	399	3.50	3.60	.50–.75
Cincinnati	6	4	13	89	112	[9] 3.35	[9] 3.35	[9] .95–.98
Chicago	12	22	20	237	384	[10] 3.40–3.60	[10] 3.25–3.35	[10] 1.00–1.10
St. Louis	8	8	6	54	92	[10] 2.75	[10] 2.75–2.90	[10] .95
Kansas City	4	1	7	62	60	[11] 2.00–2.25	[11] 2.00–2.25	[10] 1.10

[1] Carlot sales.
[2] North Dakota and Minnesota Red River Ohios.
[3] Michigan Baldwins.
[4] Missouri and Illinois Winesaps.
[5] Northwestern Extra Fancy Stayman Winesaps.
[6] Red varieties.
[7] Barrels.
[8] Texas new stock, Flat and Round-types.
[9] Bulk per 100 pounds.
[10] Tennessee Nancy Halls.
[11] Arkansas Nancy Halls.

Carlot Prices of Fruits and Vegetables at Shipping Points.

March 17, 1924, with Comparisons.

Product.	Shipping point.	Unit of sale.	Mar. 17, 1924.	Mar. 10, 1924.	Mar. 19, 1923.
Potatoes:					
Red River Ohios.	Minneapolis points.	1 0 0 pounds sacked.	[1]$0. 95–1. 00	[1]$1. 00–1. 05	$0. 85
R o u n d Whites.	Rochester, N. Y.	.....do.......	1. 35–1. 40	1. 35–1. 40	1. 45–1. 55
Do....	Grand Rapids, Mich.	.....do.......	. 90– . 98	. 90– . 98	. 87– . 90
Do....	Waupaca, Wis.	.....do...../.	1. 00	1. 05–1. 08	. 95
Rurals.....	Idaho Falls, Idaho.	.....do.......	. 90	. 75	....
G r e e n Mountains	Presque Isle, Me.	1 0 0 pounds bulk.	1. 45	1. 48–1. 53	1. 45–1. 50
Apples:					
Winesaps..	Spokane, Wash.	Boxes..........	1. 55	1. 25–1. 30	....
Baldwins..	Rochester, N. Y.	Barrels........	3. 50–3. 60		3. 75 5. 00–5. 25
Cabbage:					
Flat and Round.	San Benito, Tex.	Bulk per ton..	25. 00–28. 00	25. 00–27. 00	....
Celery:					
Golden Self-blanching.	Sanford, Fla...	10-inch crates (4–8 dozen stalks).	2. 75	2. 25–2. 50	1. 50–1. 60
Lettuce:					
I c e b e r g Type.	E l C e n t r o, Calif.	Crates.........	3. 00–3. 50	1. 50–1. 55	1. 40–1. 65

[1] U. S. No. 1 and partly graded.

Idaho Russets in Demand.

As the potato season progressed, the market position of Idaho Russets has strengthened, in accordance with anticipations last fall, when the shortage of the California crop became apparent. Since at least half of Idaho's late crop is Russets, this has induced a more optimistic feeling among growers after the depressingly low prices of recent years. Minimum autumn price in wagonloads was 75¢ per 100 lbs., according to reports from the Idaho Falls field station of the Federal market news service. There has since been a continuous advance until $1.25 was reached the first week in March, with some best stock as high as $1.35–$1.40. Rurals, which go mostly to the Southwest and Middle West, sold the first week of March at 65¢–70¢ per 100 pounds in wagonload lots, 20¢ to 25¢ above last fall's lowest range.

Quality and appearance of the Idaho Russet have facilitated its distribution from coast to coast. The "Russet Baker" is a potato term gradually becoming as well known in New York City as in Chicago and Los Angeles. One concern in the Central West is packing Idaho Russets in 15 and 30-pound cartons and, after advertising considerably during the winter, appears to be building up a good demand for high-quality stock in this unique package.

Although the movement of Rurals to California has been much greater than last season, it is apparent that Russets comprise more than 90% of Idaho's shipments to that State. Idaho had sent about 1,900 cars to California up to April 30, 1923, whereas the movement to the end of February this season had reached the 3,000 mark. Over 600 cars of Idahos were shipped to California during February alone. Thus, while this section is handicapped by high freight rates, the soil, climate altitude, and irrigation facilities produce a potato that competes successfully with stock from States closer to the great centers of population.

Idaho Russets, U. S. No. 1 grade, have been selling on the Chicago market this winter at a premium of 70¢–$1 per 100 pounds over all other varieties, and reports indicate that the California Burbank is the only competing potato bringing a higher price. During February, growers sold No. 2 Russets as high as and sometimes higher than best U. S. No. 1's a year ago.

While the crop this season was estimated at three million bushels less than the 1922 crop, increased movement has been caused chiefly by the California demand. Some 12,000 cars had been shipped by March 15, exceeding the output to the same time last season by 2,000 cars. Local estimates indicate that shipments for the entire season will total 13,500 to 14,000 cars, assuming that 2,000 to 2,500 remained after March 5. Some estimates exceed this figure, because of the quantity of No. 2's that may be marketed this spring. The final total, however, will probably be around 14,000 cars, compared with 16,213 last season.

The Yakima Valley in Washington, with a freight rate of 36½¢ by rail and boat to San Francisco, ships many Russets to California, and, as Idaho's rate is 56½¢, the movement to northern California was limited during the period of heaviest shipments from Yakima. It was estimated locally on March

1 that the Yakima Valley had less than 1,000 carloads on hand, of which a large share would be required for Portland, Oregon; Seattle, and other points on the Puget Sound. It is possible, therefore, that the extreme West will yet have to look to Idaho for its spring potato supply. The prolonged drought in California and the Japanese labor situation may permit an even greater outlet for Idaho's 1924 crop.

Water Shortage in Southern California.

Shortage of irrigation water in southern California up to March 1 resulted in a rather serious outlook for the fruit and vegetable crops usually grown there. Total rainfall in Los Angeles to February 26 was 1.82 inches, compared with 10.77 inches average and with a total seasonal average of 15.64 inches. During the first week of March, however, more than an inch of rain fell in southern California, and there was considerable snow in the mountains. Last season was below normal, with 7.28 inches of rainfall to February 26. The Imperial Valley alone is sure of a normal supply, as water for that district comes from the Colorado River.

Growers in the San Fernando Valley get their supply of irrigation water from the Los Angeles aqueduct, but, because of light local rainfall and a subnormal amount of snow in the mountains, the city had refused to allow the lands to be flooded for planting. According to advices from the Federal market reporter in Los Angeles, a few hundred acres of potatoes had been planted in dry ground, entirely at the growers' risk, in the hope of obtaining water within the next few weeks. Ordinarily from 5,000 to 8,000 acres are planted in the San Fernando section between February 15 and March 15, but less than 1,000 acres were expected this season. It is considered unsafe to plant potatoes in that district after March 15, because of danger from tuber moth in late summer.

Tomatoes need not be planted until about April 1, and will require less water than potatoes. Generous rains would increase the sizes of many small unmarketable Navel oranges on the trees, but the crop is fairly well made by this time. Within the next month, sizes of the Valencia crop will be determined. Spring lettuce was mostly planted by the end of February, and appeared to be less than last season. Deciduous fruit prospects were not bright. Although grapes are not expected to suffer severely, some of the newer vineyards are said to be on unsuitable ground.

Plantings of potatoes in Kern County are estimated locally to be about as heavy as last year. San Diego County is reported to have about 1,000 acres and San Bernardino and Riverside 1,000 acres.

There is a shortage of water all over California south of San Francisco and the Delta. In some sections, depending on wells, the water level was 5 to 10 feet below normal. Even if the wells do not go dry, this lowering requires more power for pumping, and light snowfall in the mountains has caused a shortage of power. A large electric company ordered three units for producing power from oil engines; the first of these was shipped by express at great transportation expense. The situation was serious and was depressing business. Extensive crop failures were feared. Little rain usually falls after April 1, so that another month of drought would result in shortage of water and electric power during the summer. The situation was somewhat relieved, however, by the rainfall early in March, and growers were enabled to plant a limited acreage in lettuce, potatoes, and beans.

Near San Diego the long drought has done much harm and caused growers considerable anxiety. The rainy season should have begun about two months ago, but there was practically no rain to the end of February. Many winter vegetables, including cauliflower, are grown by means of the winter rains, without irrigation. The effect of drought on these products shows in the inferior quality of offerings. Most celery in that district is grown without irrigation, and dealers attribute the large amount of black heart to dry weather. In the Chula Vista section lemon trees were heavily loaded with fruit, which is, however, small in size. There was a large amount of tree-ripe fruit.

Passings of fruits and vegetables at Potomac Yards, Va., are very heavy during winter and spring months. Recently 20 different products, chiefly from Florida, were reported to the United States Department of Agriculture. These reports of daily passings included oranges, grapefruit, celery, cabbage, tomatoes, potatoes, peas, radishes, eggplant, strawberries, spinach, romaine, chicory, string beans, peppers, escarole, sweet potatoes, apples, lettuce, and mixed vegetables.

Dairy and Poultry

Butter Market Steady But No Real Strength Apparent.

The firmer feeling which developed the latter part of the previous week was carried over into the week ending March 15 and the market closed steady. There was nothing, however, to indicate any real strength as speculative demand was almost entirely lacking. Consumptive buying lacked confidence and buyers were not inclined to anticipate their future requirements. Interest was principally on the medium and lower grades, which at the close were fairly well cleaned up on all markets. Supplies of top scores were liberal at all times and receivers very generally offered these freely in an effort to keep floor stocks as light as possible, because they believed that letting butter accumulate promised small rewards at the risk of heavier losses.

Trading stocks on the four markets were lighter than the previous week and these were comprised principally of the better grades with receivers quite generally reporting considerable improvement in quality of current arrivals. Receipts at the four markets were relatively light. In spite of these conditions, however, receivers were reluctant to advance their prices.

PRODUCTION UNCERTAIN.

Available reports gave no clear indication of either a decrease or increase in production, and consequently the production factor was of uncertain effect. The American Creamery Butter Manufacturers' Association report for the week ending March 8 showed an increase of 4.4% over the same week last year and a decrease of 4.7% compared with the preceding week this year. However, the decrease may be discounted somewhat by the fact that the make for the week of February 25 to March 1 was unusually heavy on account of arrivals of storm delayed cream. The Minnesota cooperative Creamery Association, Inc., reported an increase for the week ending March 8 of 2.039% over the previous week. As mild weather may be expected at this season of year, the possibility of an increase in receipts still hung over the market.

IMPORTS LIGHT.

During the week under review 2,584 boxes of Argentine butter from England, 2,204 casks of Danish, 150 casks of Holland, and 560 casks of Swedish butter arrived at New York. Although these imports were comparatively light, they were somewhat larger than was expected and at the moment had a slight weakening effect on the New York market. Information available on possible future imports indicated that with the exception of considerable quantities of Argentine butter due later in the month little foreign butter is slated to arrive. However, about 22,000 to 24,000 boxes of New Zealand butter are reported due the first week in April.

Cheese Trade Improves at Western Primary Markets.

During the week ending March 15 considerable improvement was noted in the volume of business at western primary cheese markets. While few dealers were willing to call trading active, all described business as better than for some time. Throughout the week the tone of the market held steady and price changes were negligible. The fact that for the past two weeks markets held practically at the same level in itself apparently added confidence on the part of both seller and buyer.

CONFIDENCE LACKING AT DISTRIBUTING POINTS.

Distributing markets, however, were in no better shape than at the close of the preceding week. With practically all conditions in the buyer's favor, lack of confidence was evident on every hand. Dealers were free sellers at inside prices or even at concessions and buyers were critical. Irregularity was prominent, the Chicago market being described as steady and eastern markets as easy. At the former trade was quiet and at the latter dull. It was difficult to ascribe the lack of confidence to any definite factor. Demand on the part of wholesale grocers and retailers was sluggish, it was true, thus indicating that possibly consumer demand was not all it should be at this time of year, due perhaps to failure of retailers to conform to wholesalers' price reductions and to availability of cheap alternatives. Receipts were heavy in spite of rumors that many factories had turned to the manufacture of butter or milk products, and storage holdings were large and showing only small reductions at a season of the year when the reverse might be expected.

At the same time, however, conditions existed which indicated a somewhat more healthy tone than did the factors described above. Prices were at a low point. Further reductions would merely result in speculative interest and immediate return to the former level. Comparison with butter and fluid milk prices further indicated that cheese prices were low. Storage stocks, while heavy as a whole, were limited to fancy goods. In addition, much of the sentimental weakness contributing to the lack of confidence was being overcome by the holding of primary markets on a steady, even basis. Thus, although the markets were quiet and unsettled, there was strength as well as weakness in the situation.

Dairy and Poultry Products at Five Markets.

(New York, Chicago, Philadelphia, Boston, and San Francisco.)

	Mar. 10–15, 1924.	Mar. 3–8, 1924.	Mar. 12–17, 1923.
Butter:	*Pounds.*	*Pounds.*	*Pounds.*
Receipts for week	12,001,885	12,070,020	10,190,651
Receipts since Jan. 1	119,775,328	107,773,443	116,631,985
Put into cold storage	499,736	852,903	2,321,839
Withdrawn from cold storage	841,006	900,601	1,026,170
Change during week	−341,270	−47,698	+1,295,660
Total holdings	4,871,196	5,212,466	5,781,395
Cheese:			
Receipts for week	3,930,930	4,103,185	2,957,404
Receipts since Jan. 1	38,763,780	34,832,850	33,922,353
Put into cold storage	402,433	565,617	473,581
Withdrawn from cold storage	1,334,892	1,457,907	1,357,952
Change during week	−932,459	−892,290	−884,371
Total holdings	12,173,802	13,106,261	6,551,383
Dressed poultry:			
Receipts for week	5,131,052	5,419,139	4,180,842
Receipts since Jan. 1	76,468,461	71,337,409	78,163,042
Put into cold storage	1,643,571	1,657,146	1,675,031
Withdrawn from cold storage	4,385,491	4,346,239	3,349,420
Change during week	−2,741,920	−2,689,093	−1,674,389
Total holdings	59,815,837	62,557,757	76,585,085
Eggs:	*Cases.*	*Cases.*	*Cases.*
Receipts for week	326,761	351,064	467,683
Receipts since Jan. 1	2,451,273	2,124,512	2,830,821
Put into cold storage	17,443	14,638	11,833
Withdrawn from cold storage	9,433	19,096	1,101
Change during week	+8,010	−4,458	+10,732
Total holdings	28,378	20,368	19,276

Wholesale Prices of Butter and Cheese.

For Week ending March 15, 1924.

(Prices Quoted in Cents per Pound.)

Creamery Butter (92 Score).

	New York.	Chicago.	Philadelphia.	Boston.	San Francisco.
Monday	48½	47	48½	49	44
Tuesday	48¾	46½	49	49	45
Wednesday	48½	46¾	49	49	44¾
Thursday	48¼	47	48	49	44¾
Friday	48½	47½	48	49	45½
Saturday	48¼	47	48½	49	45¼
Average for week	48.46	47.04	48.50	49.00	44.83
Previous week	48.04	46.50	48.08	48.92	45.00
Corresponding week last year	49.42	49.29	49.75	51.17	41.62

American Cheese. (No. 1 Fresh Twins.)

	New York.[1]	Chicago.	Boston.	San Francisco.[1]	Wisconsin.
Monday	21–21½	20–20½	22–23	22½	20½
Tuesday	21–21½	20–20½	22–23	22½	------
Wednesday	21–21½	20–20½	22–23	23	20½
Thursday	21–21½	20–20½	22–23	23	------
Friday	21–21½	20–20½	22–23	23¼	20¾
Saturday	21–21½	20–20½	22–23	23¼	------
Average for week	21.75	20.25	22.50	22.92	20.58
Previous week	21.75	20.25	22.67	22.08	20.75
Corresponding week last year	25.58	23.35	26.50	22.54	22.75

[1] Flats.

Wholesale Prices of Centralized Butter (90 Score) at Chicago.

	Cents per lb.		Cents per lb.
Monday	47	Friday	47½
Tuesday	48	Saturday	47
Wednesday	46¾–47		
Thursday	47–47¼	Average	47.21

Hay

Hay Market Stronger.

The hay market remained generally firm during the week March 10–15. Inadequate receipts of good hay caused a slight reaction from the recent downward trend and at the close prices were slightly higher than a week ago.

The supply of good hay during the week was limited at practically all markets and prices on these grades closed slightly higher. The average price of No. 1 timothy at 14 markets being $26.75 per ton. This firmness was also reflected in the lower grades and some advances in prices were noted, although some markets still were overstocked with this kind of hay. The average price for No. 2 timothy at the same markets was $24.50 per ton.

Receipts at most markets east of the Mississippi River were curtailed because of bad weather and because farmers were busy preparing for their spring work. Receipts are expected to continue small until farmers have finished their spring planting.

Boston continued overstocked with medium and low grade hay from Canada and Maine, for which there was little demand. Receivers cut prices in order to save storage charges but this did not stimulate buying so the hay accumulated in the railroad sheds.

The light receipts and improved demand at New York caused buyers from Brooklyn and the Bronx to go to Manhattan for supplies. Good hay in large bales was in active demand. The decreased receipts and the probability of a further curtailment as spring approaches, together with an expected good demand from buyers who would want to increase their stocks to carry them through the period of light country movement had a strengthening influence on the market at Cincinnati. Timothy receipts at Kansas City exceeded the demand and prices declined a little towards the last of the week.

There was a heavier movement of hay to Kansas City from the producing areas of the Southwest and West. With the approach of spring and a good outlook for pasturage producers are shipping their surplus stocks. The best grades of alfalfa were in good demand from the dairy trade, but ordinary varieties sold slowly. The demand from the South and Southwest was not as good as in previous weeks, nor were they buying in the volume that is ordinarily usual at this season.

The eastern demand for alfalfa at Omaha increased during the week. There was a good demand for green leafy alfalfa at Minneapolis during the week from local trade and from shippers, but the receipts were not sufficient to supply even the local trade.

The increased demand for alfalfa caused by the drought in California has consumed all available hay in the Salt River Valley of Arizona, and the carryover in this section will be light. The first cutting is expected during April.

Best grades of prairie were in good demand, while lower grades moved slowly. There was some demand from the South and Southeast at Kansas City, but not enough to absorb the offerings. Stockyards there bought on a very small scale. The prairie market at Omaha was a little stronger, and the best grades moved more freely as the demand from the east for spring feeding increased.

Prairie hay was in good demand toward the last of the week in Chicago because of the scarcity of timothy; however, only the top grades were wanted.

There was a good demand for hay at Minneapolis, and practically all grades of prairie sold well. The average price of No. 1 prairie at five of the principal markets was $16.50 per ton.

Receipts for the week with comparisons follow:

	Mar. 10 to Mar. 15, 1924.	Mar. 3 to Mar. 8, 1924.	Mar. 12 to Mar. 17, 1923.	Jan. 1 to Mar. 15, 1924.	Jan. 1 to Mar. 15, 1923.
	Cars.	Cars.	Cars.	Cars.	Cars.
Boston	61	87	125	893	907
New York	159	190	227	2,292	1,620
Philadelphia	54	45	43	815	804
Pittsburgh	145	136	75	1,500	1,338
Cincinnati	88	149	125	1,463	1,495
Chicago	196	311	245	3,292	2,380
Minneapolis-St. Paul	95	141	144	1,076	1,385
St. Louis	186	145	153	1,667	1,941
Omaha	140	160	189	1,682	1,531
Kansas City	705	637	428	6,800	5,494
Los Angeles	284	250	200	2,748	1,532
San Francisco	104	92	76	1,399	834

Market for Hops in Switzerland.

Switzerland offers a good market for American hops, says Consul G. Willrich at St. Gall. Hitherto most of the hops imported by Switzerland came from Bohemia, Bavaria, and Wurtemberg. The present time seems to be most propitious for the introduction of the American product because the 1923 European crop was small and a shortage in production is expected again in 1924. The selection of a first class representative of American hop growers in Switzerland must be the first step to insure large sales, says the consul. Such a man should be located in Zurich. A first class representative in Zurich should be able to start his campaign for the introduction of American hops within a few months to effect successful sales for 1924–25. The name of a suitable agent at Zurich will be supplied upon request by the American consul stationed at Zurich. According to the Swiss Federal Customs Department, that country imported 750 thousand pounds of hops during 1922.

Carload Prices of Hay and Straw, Per Ton, at Important Markets, March 15, 1924.

Commodity.	Boston.[1]	New York.[1 2]	Philadelphia.[1 2]	Pittsburgh[1]	Richmond.[2]	Atlanta.	Savannah.	New Orleans.	Memphis.[1]	Cincinnati.[1]	Chicago.[1 2]	Minneapolis and St. Paul.[1 2]	St. Louis.[1]	Omaha.[1]	Kansas City.[1]	Los Angeles.[1]	San Francisco.[1]
HAY.																	
Timothy and clover:																	
No. 1 timothy	[3]$28.00	$30.50	$28.00	$26.00	$28.00	$30.00	$32.50	$29.00	$28.50	$24.50	$26.00	$19.50	$25.50		$19.00		
No. 2 timothy	[3] 25.00	28.50	27.00	24.00	27.00	29.00	30.00	27.75	24.50	23.50	21.50	17.50	22.00		13.75		
No. 1 light clover mixed		28.00	27.00	25.00	27.50	29.50	31.00			23.50	24.00	18.00			18.50		
No. 2 light clover mixed		25.00	25.00		26.00	28.50					20.50	16.50					
No. 1 medium clover mixed			25.00		27.00						21.00						
No. 1 clover mixed	[3] 21.00			26.00						23.00		[3] 17.50			16.75		
No. 1 clover				26.00	28.00					24.00	21.00	[3] 19.50	23.50		19.00		
Alfalfa:																	
No. 1 alfalfa		31.50			32.00	25.00		31.50	30.00	28.50	28.00	22.00	28.00	$19.50	24.50	$29.00	$26.00
Standard alfalfa					30.00	32.00		29.50	27.50	26.50	22.00	18.00		16.50	21.00	26.00	25.00
No. 2 alfalfa						29.00			21.00	21.00	18.00	15.00	18.00	13.75	18.00		24.00
Prairie:																	
No. 1 upland								17.50			19.00	16.50		13.25	14.00		
No. 2 upland											17.00	15.00		11.00	12.00		
No. 1 midland											12.00	12.00	18.50	12.50			
STRAW.																	
No. 1 wheat	11.50		18.00	15.50	15.00	11.00			14.00	11.00	7.00		7.50	6.75			
No. 1 oat	13.50	15.00	18.00	15.50		11.00			14.00	11.00	8.00		8.50	6.75			
No. 1 rye	[4] 24.00	[4] 22.00	20.00	16.00					16.00	13.00	8.50						

[1] Hay quotations represent average of cash sales at these markets.   [2] Hay quotations based on U. S. Grades.   [3] Nominal.   [4] Straight.

Grain

Grain Market Weaker.

The recent estimate of the Department of Agriculture which indicated larger farm stocks of grain than were generally expected by the trade were a depressing factor in the grain market and prices on all grains suffered material declines during the week March 10–15.

May wheat declined about 3½¢ and closed at Chicago at $1.06¼. July wheat made similar declines, closing at $1.07⅛. May and July corn future prices were also a little more than 3¢ lower than the May at Chicago, closing at 77½¢ with July at 78¾¢. Oats future prices were down about 1¢ at Chicago, closing at 46⅛¢. The stocks of wheat on farms on March 1 were estimated at 133,871,000 bushels, or 17% of the 1923 crop, as against 155,474,000 bushels, or 17.9% of the 1922 crop on farms March 1. The reduction of 21⅗ million bushels over last year, however, was less than generally expected by the trade and caused some liquidation in the future market as well as some short selling. The stocks in mills were estimated at 90,396,000 bushels, which was about 2 million bushels less than at the corresponding time last year. The visible supply, however, continues around 16,000,000 bushels larger than last year and exports for the crop year to date have been only about two-thirds of the amount exported for the corresponding period last year.

	Wheat.		Corn.		Oats	
	Mar. 10-15.	Mar. 3-8.	Mar. 10-15.	Mar. 3-8.	Mar. 10-15.	Mar. 3-8.
	Bushels.	*Bushels.*	*Bushels.*	*Bushels.*	*Bushels.*	*Bushels.*
Primary receipts	4,689,000	4,715,000	7,492,000	10,674,000	4,349,000	5,519,000
Primary receipts last year	5,899,000	6,074,000	6,018,000	7,998,000	4,584,000	4,081,000
Primary shipments	2,959,000	3,185,000	3,985,000	4,812,000	3,686,000	3,584,000
Primary shipments last year	2,919,000	3,234,000	3,879,000	4,133,000	4,672,000	3,941,000
Visible supply	61,656,000	62,406,000	25,052,000	22,457,000	18,063,000	18,023,000
Visible supply last year	46,470,000	46,581,000	30,540,000	29,730,000	25,325,000	26,208,000
	Cars.	*Cars.*	*Cars.*	*Cars.*	*Cars.*	*Cars.*
Chicago	223	255	830	1,634	421	845
Minneapolis	1,576	1,339	404	504	203	285
Duluth	406	341	248	624	41	56
St. Louis	298	356	457	451	311	386
Kansas City	609	618	582	481	106	126
Omaha	217	217	717	609	123	147
Cincinnati	51	97	74	162	41	65
Indianapolis	29	[1] 53	187	[1] 439	99	[1] 149
Toledo	119	164	74	132	42	66
Milwaukee	21	29	338	730	116	182
Wichita	204	235	135	120	9	14
Hutchinson	82	101	------	------	------	------
Sioux City [1]	17	14	71	128	48	54
Cairo [1]	------	------	258	175	257	235
Ft. Worth	94	88	59	68	14	34
St. Joseph	95	97	221	261	20	20

[1] Week ending Friday.

While the movement of wheat into commercial channels has been materially less than last year it should be noted that the consumption has been larger than usual and that if the present rate of consumption should continue during the remainder of the crop year the carryover will not be burdensome. While it is too early to determine the amount of winter wheat area that will be abandoned reports indicate that the condition of the crop December 1 was better than last year and better than the average. If the average percentage, 9.8, is abandoned and yield per acre equals the average of the last ten years production of winter wheat will be but slightly less than last year. Reports of intentions to plant in the spring wheat area show that farmers in that territory are planning to plant 14% less acreage of spring wheat, including durum in 1924 than in 1923. If these intentions are carried out production of spring wheat should keep well within domestic needs for hard red spring wheat.

Cash prices in most markets followed the general trend of future prices and ranged 3–5¢ lower at the various markets. The better milling grades of both spring and hard winter wheat were in good demand. In the spring wheat markets the cash basis was well maintained with No. 1 dark northern selling from 2–16¢ over the May future price at Minneapolis.

While mills in the hard winter territory report a rather dull flour demand there was a feeling that the supply of choice milling grades would be exhausted before the new crop becomes available. The stocks of all kinds of hard winter wheat in the principal markets, however, continue rather heavy and have been reduced slowly. This supply continues to be a depressing factor in the market, especially for the lower grades.

The red winter wheat markets were relatively weaker than for the other kinds as the demand from Southern mills was rather limited because of the small flour and feed trade in that territory. The supply of winter wheat in the mills in Virginia, Ohio, Indiana, Illinois, and Michigan was larger on March 1 than at the same period in 1923.

The advance in tariff rates which become effective early in April apparently has had but little effect upon the market up to the present time. There are, however, in the United States about 19,000,000 bushels of Canadian wheat in bond upon about two-thirds of which it might be practicable for the owners to pay the present duty and release it for milling in United States mills.

Corn prices were also lower for the week and the market was somewhat depressed by the larger stocks on farms and a slight falling off in demand at the various markets. As in wheat, however, the reports indicate larger farm consumption during the winter, but with the present tendency of farmers to reduce their hog stocks it seems probable that the feeding demand will be materially decreased later in the season. This may result in a larger carryover at the beginning of the new crop. Reports of farmers intentions to plant corn this spring indicate that they are now planning to plant an acreage about 3% larger than was harvested last year. This increase in corn acreage over 1923, if coupled with yields as good as last season's, will result in a further increase in the supply for next fall and winter.

The demand at practically all markets during the week was less urgent but reports indicate that farmers were not selling freely at the lower prices. Lower grades were relatively weaker than the better grades, especially in the markets tributary to the soft corn area. The price level is still about 5¢ higher than at the corresponding time last year but recently the spread between this year and last year prices has been narrowed materially.

The stocks of oats on farms were also larger than last year but they constituted a smaller percentage of the crop than last year, which together with the smaller receipts at the markets indicates a rather large consumption to date.

Oats prices were slightly lower with other grains and declines 1–2½¢ per bushel were reported at the various markets. The outlook, however, indicates a continued good demand for oats, especially in the Southern and Southeastern States where a large percentage of the winter oats have been killed. While some of the ground planted to winter oats will be reseeded with spring oats they will furnish but little grain and will be used principally for forage. Farmers on March 1 expressed an intention to increase their oat acreage 7% over that harvested in 1923 but both the 1923 and 1922 acreages were low compared with the acreage seemingly required for the increased numbers of livestock.

The rye market was weaker because of the small demand from shippers. Prices were 3–5¢ lower in the principal markets. The rye market has been rather unsatisfactory recently and this situation is apparently influencing farmers' intentions to harvest this crop for grain, as these intentions show a 5% reduction from the planting of last fall, which was estimated at 16% below the 1923 harvested acreage. Winter seedings of rye in 10 countries, constituting 53% of the total area seeded last year outside of Russia, show an increase of 145,000 acres.

Falling off in the demand from maltsters weakened the barley market slightly but reports indicate that the large crop produced in 1923 is being rapidly consumed. The supply on farms March 1 was about 44,800,000 bushels, which was 22.6% of the 1923 crop, which was about 16,000,000 bushels larger than the 1922 crop; 23.3% of the 1922 crop was on farms March 1, 1923.

Heavy arrivals of Argentine flax seed at eastern markets caused a sharp break in flax prices early in the week and May future prices at Minneapolis declined about 15¼¢ during the week. Flax prices, however, have been very satisfactory during the present crop year and farmers have expressed an intention of increasing their plantings over last year's harvested acreage by 54%. The consumption of flax seed in the United States is more than twice the amount usually produced, which would seem to indicate that a material increase in acreage could be made if present tariff rates are maintained. There would be the possibility, however, of the increase in acreage causing some reduction in the price level because the United States producers would have to meet the foreign price competition at the Atlantic seaboard rather than at Minneapolis, as at present.

GRAIN PRICES.

Average Prices of Wheat, Corn, and Oats at Certain Markets, December, 1922–February, 1924, Inclusive.

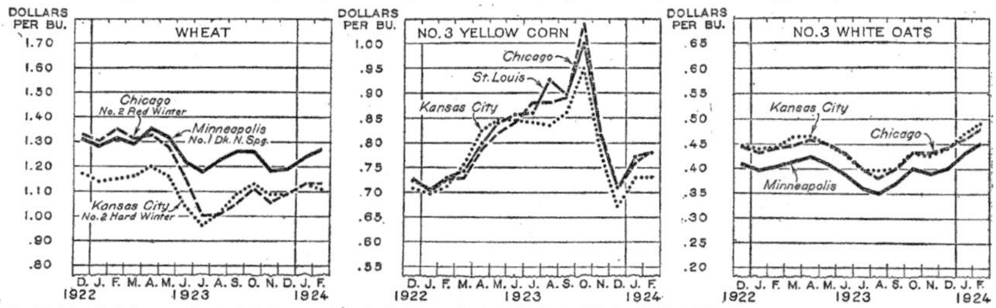
DOLLARS PER BU.
WHEAT
1.70
1.60
1.50
1.40
1.30
1.20
1.10
1.00
.90
.80
Chicago No. 2 Red Winter
Minneapolis No. 1 Dk. N. Spg.
Kansas City No. 2 Hard Winter
D. J. F. M. A. M. J. J. A. S. O. N. D. J. F.
1922 1923 1924
DOLLARS PER BU.
NO. 3 YELLOW CORN
1.00
.95
.90
.85
.80
.75
.70
.65
.60
.55
Chicago
St. Louis
Kansas City
D. J. F. M. A. M. J. J. A. S. O. N. D. J. F.
1922 1923 1924
DOLLARS PER BU.
NO. 3 WHITE OATS
.65
.60
.55
.50
.45
.40
.35
.30
.25
.20
Kansas City
Chicago
Minneapolis
D. J. F. M. A. M. J. J. A. S. O. N. D. J. F.
1922 1923 1924

Daily Weighted Price per Bushel of Reported Cash Sales at Stated Markets, Week of March 8–14, 1924, with Comparisons of Weekly Averages.

Wheat.

Market and grade.	Daily prices. Sat.	Mon.	Tues.	Wed.	Thu.	Fri.	Weekly averages. Mar. 8–14, 1923.	Mar. 1–7, 1924.	Mar. 8–14, 1924.
CHICAGO.	Cents.	Cents.	Cents.	Cents.	Cents.	Cents.	Cents.	Cents.	Cents.
Hard winter ... No. 2	114	112	113	109	108	108	119	113	111
No. 3	111	110	112	108	104	107	------	111	109
Red winter ... No. 2	112	------	------	------	------	------	131	113	112
No. 3	110	108	109	------	------	105	130	110	108
MINNEAPOLIS.									
Dk. No. Spring ... No. 1	131	130	128	128	125	126	129	127	128
No. 2	126	124	124	125	121	122	126	124	123
No. 3	121	122	118	118	117	118	118	120	119
No. Spring ... No. 1	124	123	125	121	120	118	124	123	123
No. 2	126	118	117	115	120	118	122	120	118
No. 3	113	115	116	112	114	114	118	116	114
Am. Durum ... No. 2	122	120	121	118	117	120	110	118	120
KANSAS CITY.									
Dk Hd. Winter ... No. 2	------	------	114	114	119	120	119	------	117
No. 3	------	------	112	------	------	------	118	------	112
Hd. Winter ... No. 2	110	111	110	109	107	103	115	112	109
No. 3	109	109	109	106	107	104	115	110	107
Red Winter ... No. 2	116	114	113	113	111	------	130	116	113
No. 3	113	112	111	116	109	107	126	114	111
OMAHA.									
Dk. Hd. Winter ... No. 2	------	------	------	------	------	------	117	------	------
No. 3	------	------	------	------	------	------	118	114	------
Hd. Winter ... No. 2	108	106	105	------	102	101	112	106	104
No. 3	106	108	103	105	101	100	111	106	104
ST. LOUIS.									
Hd. Winter ... No. 2	------	110	------	108	------	------	110	112	108
Red Winter ... No. 2	114	114	113	112	109	110	139	115	112
No. 3	112	112	112	------	108	107	133	113	110
FIVE MARKETS.									
All classes and grades	115	114	113	112	109	109	120	113	112

Corn.

Market and grade.	Sat.	Mon.	Tues.	Wed.	Thu.	Fri.	Mar. 8–14, 1923.	Mar. 1–7, 1924.	Mar. 8–14, 1924.
CHICAGO.									
White ... No. 2	------	------	------	81	80	------	74	------	80
No. 3	78	78	79	78	78	78	72	78	78
Yellow ... No. 2	------	------	------	81	80	------	74	82	80
No. 3	79	79	79	79	78	78	73	78	78
Mixed ... No. 2	------	------	------	------	------	------	74	------	------
No. 3	78	79	79	78	78	77	72	77	78
KANSAS CITY.									
White ... No. 2	------	------	------	------	------	------	71	76	------
No. 3	72	72	73	72	72	72	72	73	72
Yellow ... No. 2	------	------	------	------	------	73	73	74	73
No. 3	72	72	72	72	72	72	72	73	72
Mixed ... No. 2	------	------	------	------	71	70	71	74	71
No. 3	70	70	70	70	69	69	71	70	69
OMAHA.									
White ... No. 2	------	72	------	------	------	------	69	74	72
No. 3	71	71	71	70	------	69	68	71	70
Yellow ... No. 2	------	------	------	------	------	------	69	74	------
No. 3	70	71	70	71	------	69	68	70	70
Mixed ... No. 2	------	------	------	------	71	------	68	------	71
No. 3	68	68	68	69	68	67	67	68	68

Corn—Continued.

Market and grade.	Daily prices. Sat.	Mon.	Tues.	Wed.	Thu.	Fri.	Weekly averages. Mar. 1–7, 1923.	Mar. 1–7, 1924.	Mar. 8–14, 1924.
ST. LOUIS.	Cents.	Cents.	Cents.	Cents.	Cents.	Cents.	Cents.	Cents.	Cents.
White ... No. 2	------	------	------	------	------	------	74	------	------
No. 3	77	78	78	77	76	76	73	77	77
Yellow ... No. 2	------	------	------	82	------	------	74	------	82
No. 3	78	78	78	78	77	76	73	77	78
Mixed ... No. 2	------	------	------	------	------	------	74	78	------
No. 3	76	77	76	76	75	74	73	76	75
FIVE MARKETS.									
All classes and grades	72	73	74	74	72	73	72	73	73

Oats, White.

Market and grade.	Sat.	Mon.	Tues.	Wed.	Thu.	Fri.	Mar. 1–7, 1923.	Mar. 1–7, 1924.	Mar. 8–14, 1924.
CHICAGO ... No. 2	48	48	47	47	46	47	46	49	47
No. 3	47	47	47	46	45	46	44	48	46
MINNEAPOLIS ... No. 2	44	44	44	44	43	43	43	45	44
No. 3	44	44	43	43	42	42	41	44	43
KANSAS CITY ... No. 2	49	------	48	------	------	------	47	49	49
No. 3	48	48	48	47	47	47	46	48	48
OMAHA ... No. 3	46	46	46	45	45	45	43	46	45
ST. LOUIS ... No. 2	49	49	49	49	48	48	47	50	49
No. 3	48	48	48	48	47	47	46	49	48

Rye.

Market and grade.	Sat.	Mon.	Tues.	Wed.	Thu.	Fri.	Mar. 1–7, 1923.	Mar. 1–7, 1924.	Mar. 8–14, 1924.
CHICAGO ... No. 2	71	71	71	71	------	------	82	71	71
MINNEAPOLIS ... No. 2	65	65	64	64	59	60	76	65	63

Barley.

Market and grade.	Sat.	Mon.	Tues.	Wed.	Thu.	Fri.	Mar. 1–7, 1923.	Mar. 1–7, 1924.	Mar. 8–14, 1924.
MINNEAPOLIS ... No. 2	------	------	------	------	65	------	58	71	65

Closing Prices of Grain Futures, March 14, 1924, with Comparisons.

Wheat.

Market.	May futures. 1923 Mar. 7.	May futures. 1923 Mar. 14.	May futures. 1924 Mar. 7.	May futures. 1924 Mar. 14.	July futures. 1923 Mar. 7.	July futures. 1923 Mar. 14.	July futures. 1924 Mar. 7.	July futures. 1924 Mar. 14.
	Cents	Cents.	Cents.	Cents.	Cents.	Cents.	Cents.	Cents.
Chicago	118⅜	119⅜	111⅛	105⅞	114¼	114⅝	111⅝	106½
Minneapolis	119½	119½	116⅝	112¼	119	119¾	118	113⅝
Kansas City	110⅝	111⅛	105	99¼	106¾	107⅛	104¾	99½
Winnipeg	112⅞	114	103⅛	99¾	113⅜	115⅛	105	101⅝
Liverpool	133⅝	135	117⅛	115	------	134⅝	116⅛	113⅛

Corn.

Market.	May 1923 Mar. 7.	May 1923 Mar. 14.	May 1924 Mar. 7.	May 1924 Mar. 14.	July 1923 Mar. 7.	July 1923 Mar. 14.	July 1924 Mar. 7.	July 1924 Mar. 14.
Chicago	73⅞	73⅝	80⅞	77⅞	75¾	75⅝	81⅜	79⅛
Kansas City	71¾	70⅝	75⅛	73½	72⅜	72⅝	76½	74¾

Oats.

Market.	May 1923 Mar. 7.	May 1923 Mar. 14.	May 1924 Mar. 7.	May 1924 Mar. 14.	July 1923 Mar. 7.	July 1923 Mar. 14.	July 1924 Mar. 7.	July 1924 Mar. 14.
Chicago	44¾	44½	47¾	46	44¼	44⅛	46	44⅝
Winnipeg	47¾	48¼	41½	39⅞	47¾	48	42⅜	40⅞

Feed

Feedstuffs Supplies Exceed Demand.

The millfeed markets were unsettled and prices irregularly lower during the week March 8–15. There were more anxious sellers than buyers, which was not so much due to any increased output of mills as it was to an accumulation of track offerings and a fairly liberal supply of transit shipments. Generally speaking, there was no pressure to sell feed on the part of mills.

Prices received for milk by farmers were believed by retailers to be mainly responsible for the abnormally small consumptive demand. This in turn led to light sales by jobbers to the interior. On the other hand, flour mills, corn mills, and oil mills continued to enjoy a good business. The resulting surplus of feed by-products, coupled with rather heavy storage stocks, caused prices of every feed to decline.

It was the consensus of opinion among the trade that little improvement in prices can be made as long as this surplus hangs heavy on the market and that should production continue to exceed consumption still lower markets may be looked for.

Wheat millfeeds.—An extremely weak tone prevailed in the market for wheat millfeeds. An outstanding feature was a further narrowing of the spread between bran and shorts, the latter selling at only 75 cents per ton over bran, the unusual differential that has prevailed for quite some time. Southern feeders bought shorts very sparingly indicating that the normal enlargement in spring pig feeding has not yet developed. The Northwest reported middlings to be more or less a drug on the market and advices from Minneapolis and Chicago were to the effect that it was almost impossible to secure a favorable bid on this feed. Flour middlings were heavy. Despite the fact that the better known brands of this feed were offered both by mills and resellers at about bran prices they were difficult to move. Middlings were obtainable in most of the markets at 50 cents to $1 less than bran. Canadian offerings exerted little influence in the Northeast. These offerings were made at about $1 under domestic prices and were fairly well absorbed. Production was good and the output of mills was in excess of the demand. The slow disposition of storage stocks tended to depress the markets and assisted the downward movement in prices. The demand for bran from the interior was fair but was principally for nearby shipment. Deferred deliveries were quoted on a scale down, about 50 cents per ton lower for each month. The movement was good.

Cottonseed cake and meal.—Financial troubles of one of the largest chains of cotton oil mills brought a sudden stop to the better demand for cottonseed cake and meal witnessed last week. The weakness of corn also was responsible for more

hesitancy in the buying of these high protein feeds. Stocks while not excessive were fully adequate, as the eastern demand was not any too brisk and export sales were also of small volume. Offerings were liberal both by southern mills and southern and northern resellers for either shipment or transit basis. Future shipment was quoted on a par with immediate and March shipment. Fertilizer concerns and commercial mixers bought lightly. The latter complained of a sluggish demand for their balanced rations which was reflected in a slow absorption of raw feeds by this class of trade. The movement was light.

Linseed cake and meal.—The domestic demand for linseed cake and meal was light. Offerings were liberal both by mills and resellers, but resellers were the only ones pressing the market. Mills were able to obtain prevailing prices for almost any amount they cared to sell for export which tended to hold prices steady. However, at the close Buffalo quoted 34 per cent meal at $40.25, or 50–75 cents lower than last week. Production was good. The movement was about the average for this time of the year. Shipments from Minneapolis continued good and were 4,432,051 pounds during the week compared to 4,212,223 pounds during the previous week.

Gluten feed.—The demand for gluten feed was slow. Offerings were liberal both by mills and resellers, particularly the latter, who discounted the mills prices in order to move what they purchased at the recent low prices. In the Northeast stocks were not moved as easily as was expected and a number of the small manufacturers shaded their price $1 per ton from that quoted by the larger mills. The latter quoted unchanged from last week with the usual guaranty against decline on date of arrival of shipments. Production was heavy and stocks generally were good. The reduction of $3 per ton in gluten meal last week was said to have resulted in a substantial increase in sales of this feed. The movement was good.

Hominy feed.—Hominy feed was offered more freely and prices were barely sustained. A number of sales were reported at discounts from ruling prices in sympathy with the decline in the coarse grain. Yellow and white hominy feed were quoted at the same figure in a number of markets. This was due to the fact that plenty of white hominy feed was to be had while yellow hominy was rather scarce. Shipping instructions were difficult to secure and mills with limited storage capacity pressed sales to the utmost in order to move their stocks. Interior supplies were good and the movement was heavy.

Alfalfa meal.—While offerings of alfalfa meal from Colorado and other Western States were considerably smaller than last week the markets for this feed were weaker as a result of plentiful supplies and the absence of a substantial demand. Meal in some instances was sold at less than production cost. This condition it was thought by the trade would not last very long, as grinders no doubt will resell their holdings of alfalfa hay rather than lose money by grinding it. Choice meal was quoted at $31 in the Chicago market and fine ground No. 1 meal sold at $30 per ton in Kansas City. The movement was good.

Carload Prices of Feedstuffs at Important Markets, March 15, 1924.

[Per ton, bagged, sight-draft basis.]

Commodity.	Boston.	Philadelphia.	Pittsburgh.	Baltimore.	Atlanta.	Savannah.	Memphis.	Cincinnati.	Buffalo.	Chicago.	Minneapolis.	St. Louis.	Omaha.	Kansas City.	Los Angeles.	San Francisco.
Wheat bran:																
Spring	$30.50	$30.00	$29.50	$31.50	$33.50			$28.50	$27.00	$24.50	$21.50					
Soft winter	33.75	33.00	32.50	32.50	33.50	$34.50	$28.00	29.50	30.50			$26.00		$24.00		
Hard winter	32.50	32.00	31.00		33.00		28.00	28.50	30.00	27.00		26.00	$23.75	24.00		$31.00
Wheat middlings:																
Spring (standard)	30.25	29.50	28.50	31.50	34.50			28.50	27.00	24.25	21.00					
Soft winter	36.50	36.00	32.00	32.00	35.00	35.50	29.00	31.00	34.00			28.00		25.00		39.00
Hard winter			32.50		34.00			31.00	33.00			28.00	27.00	26.00		
Hard winter wheat shorts					34.50		28.00		33.00				25.00	24.00		32.00
Wheat millrun	32.25	31.50			34.00						23.00			24.50	$30.00	30.00
Rye middlings	29.50	29.00	27.00								19.00					
High protein meals:																
Linseed	45.50	44.25	45.50					46.00	41.00	41.00	41.00	43.50	46.00	45.00		45.00
Cottonseed (43%)	50.25	49.00	47.00	48.00			41.50	46.50	48.25	46.00	47.00	45.00	45.00	43.25		49.00
Cottonseed (41%)	47.00	47.00	46.00	45.50			39.50	44.50	46.75	44.50	45.50	43.00		42.50		
Cottonseed (36%)	43.00	45.00	43.00	42.05	37.00	38.00	36.50	40.50	43.25	41.50	43.50	39.75				
Digester feeding tankage (60%)											50.00	50.00	50.00	50.00		
No. 1 alfalfa meal (medium)							25.00	26.50				23.00	23.00	25.00	34.00	
Gluten feed	41.55	40.50	38.30	39.50				37.30	38.30	34.40						
White hominy feed	35.25	34.50		35.00	36.50			31.50	32.00	29.00		28.00	27.00			
Yellow hominy feed	34.25	33.50		34.00	36.50			31.50	31.50	29.00			27.00			
Ground barley								36.00		36.50				$40.00		
Dried beet pulp			32.25	38.00		42.00		37.00	36.00	34.50				38.00		37.00

[1] Rolled.

Seeds

Clover and Alfalfa Seed Demand Good.

Red and alsike clover and alfalfa seed prices advanced with the increased demand for these seeds during the week March 10–15. Other seeds were in fairly good demand and prices, although mostly unchanged, were firmer with but few exceptions. In many sections of the Middle West and East the soil was too wet for sowing. As soon as it dries out sufficiently more activity is expected in the seed business.

Clovers and alfalfa.—Red and alsike clover prices were up 25¢–50¢ per 100 lbs. from quotations of the preceding week in a number of markets. The demand for these seeds was good. Arrivals of red clover, subject to the seed importation act, fell off further during the past week, about 780,000 lbs. being received at New York and Baltimore from Great Britain, France, Chile, and Holland. Approximately 45,000 lbs. of alsike clover was exported from New York to Great Britain.

Alfalfa prices were higher in a majority of markets, advances of as much as $1–$1.50 being recorded for a few markets. No alfalfa was received at New York or Baltimore from foreign countries during the week. Rumors afloat in the East and Middle West to the effect that an increase in the duty on alfalfa seed from 4¢ to 10¢ were without foundation.

There is no demand for crimson clover. White clover demand has been fair. About 4,400 lbs. of white clover arrived at New York from Germany.

Sweet clover prices were mostly unchanged but were considered to be decidedly firmer because of increases in clover and alfalfa prices.

Grasses.—Timothy demand was only fair and prices were a trifle weaker but remained at last week's levels. Approximately 108,000 lbs. of timothy was exported from New York to Germany and Great Britain. The continued fair export demand has tended to maintain timothy prices.

Redtop and Kentucky bluegrass were in fairly good demand and prices were firm. Orchard grass demand has been fair at prices considerably higher than last year. Meadow fescue prices have remained at the same level since the opening of the season. The European demand apparently has not come up to expectations.

Miscellaneous seeds.—Millet market was dull and no important price changes occurred. German and Hungarian millet prices have shown more strength than prices for other varieties.

Sorgo demand was listless and prices were a little weaker in the Missouri Valley.

Sudan grass prices were barely maintained in producing sections although present wholesale prices are about $4 lower than last year on a corresponding date.

No unusual activity in the cowpea and soy bean market was noted. Some Central Western points are continuing to have difficulty in obtaining supplies of high germinating cowpeas.

Seed corn demand was a little better during the past week. Many seedsmen are offering 1922 instead of 1923 corn because of better germination.

Approximately 132,000 lbs. of rape from Holland, France, and Germany, 11,200 lbs. of rye grass from Great Britain, and 55,000 lbs. of vetch from Holland and Germany arrived at New York during the week.

Austria to Import Frozen Beef.

As a means of terminating the steady rise in the price of meat in Vienna, the Austrian price control office is actively encouraging the importation of first-class frozen beef, says P. M. Terry, American trade commissioner at that post. A cooperative society has been formed to handle imports from North and South America and from Australia. Frozen meat is a novelty on the Viennese market and it will have to overcome a serious prejudice on the part of the consuming population. The Government is confident, however, that the Viennese will willingly purchase frozen meat if it is of first quality and is offered at advantageous prices.

Wholesale Prices of Field Seeds, March 15, 1924.

For Best Grades of Seed Offered by Seedsmen, with Purity and Germination Tests Approximately as Indicated.

[Per 100 pounds, except seed grains, which are per bushel.]

Kind of seed.	Average test.		New York.	Balti-more.	Rich-mond.	Buf-falo.	Toledo.	Louis-ville.	Chica-go.	Min-ne-apolis.	St. Louis.	Kansas City.	Den-ver.	Salt Lake City.	Average for U. S., Mar. 17 1923.	Average for U. S. Mar. 18, 1922.
	Purity.	Germina-tion.														
	P. ct.	P. ct.														
Clovers:																
Red clover	99.4	92	$20.75	$20.50	$22.50	$22.50	$20.25	$22.00	$21.75	$25.00	$23.75	$24.00	$22.00	$22.00	$21.00	$25.65
Alsike clover	98.3	91	15.50	16.00	17.00	15.50	15.25	16.00	15.50	17.00	16.00	18.00	17.00	16.00	17.45	19.95
White clover	96.9	91	49.00	49.00	50.00	50.00	50.00	50.00	45.00	52.50	49.00	50.00	50.00	45.00	59.35	40.15
Crimson clover	98.2	91	9.00	8.00	8.00	9.75			9.00						17.65	11.35
Sweet clover	98.9	90	15.00	14.50	15.00	14.50	15.00	16.00	14.25	15.50	15.00	18.00	18.00		12.40	9.25
Lespedeza	98.9	82		23.00	21.50			19.50			23.00				20.40	18.70
Alfalfa	99.5	91	20.50	20.50	20.50	22.50	23.00	20.50	22.50	24.50	20.50	23.00	21.00	22.00	19.80	19.15
Grasses:																
Timothy	99.6	93	8.50	8.50	8.75	8.65	8.35	8.50	8.15	8.40	8.25	8.50	9.00	8.50	7.30	7.35
Redtop	93.2	90	14.00	14.00	15.00	14.75	16.00	13.75	13.50	15.00	14.25	13.00	18.00		20.20	24.50
Kentucky bluegrass	83	78	25.50	23.50	26.50	26.00	26.50	28.50	24.75	26.00	27.00	25.00	26.00	27.50	25.25	22.05
Orchard grass	86.9	87	17.50	17.50	16.50	18.00	18.00	17.00	16.75	20.00	18.00	17.50	18.00		13.85	18.90
Meadow fescue	97.8	91	11.00		13.50	12.00	12.00		11.00	12.50		10.50	11.00		10.85	19.45
Millets:																
German millet	98.8	93		5.50	4.75		5.00		4.00	4.50	4.00	3.25	3.00		4.25	2.55
Common millet	98	93	3.50		3.00				2.50	2.75	2.00	1.90	3.60		3.55	2.25
Siberian millet	97.9	93							2.40	2.75	2.00	1.90	3.60		3.85	2.25
Hungarian millet	97.5	93	4.75		4.00				4.00	4.00	4.00				3.60	3.05
Japanese millet	96.4	89	3.50		2.75				2.50	2.75		4.00			3.10	4.35
Broomcorn millet	99.3	92							2.10	2.50	2.00	2.60	2.50		3.75	2.55
Sorgo ("Cane"):																
Amber sorgo	97.9	88		3.50		5.00	3.00		2.25	3.00	2.00	1.70	2.00		4.75	2.55
Orange sorgo	97.9	88		3.50			3.00				2.45	1.95	3.00		5.25	2.70
Grain sorghums:																
Kafir	98.1	91		3.25							2.25	1.85	3.00		2.95	2.35
Milo	97.7	91		3.25							2.55	2.10	3.00		2.90	2.45
Sudan grass	98.0	91		11.50	10.50	10.00	10.00	10.00	10.00	9.00	10.00	9.00		14.40	4.30
Rape	99.2	92	5.75	3.50	5.75	6.50	6.75	6.25	6.00	6.50	6.00	6.75	7.00		7.20	7.85
Vetches:																
Hairy vetch	98.7	89	10.00	10.50	12.00	11.75			10.50		15.00	16.50		19.00		17.85	13.80
Common vetch	98.7	92	4.25	4.00	8.00	5.50	7.00			7.50			9.00		7.40	6.25
Peas:																
Canada field peas	99.3	95	5.00	5.00	5.25	4.90	5.25		4.85	5.00	5.00	6.00			5.45	5.00
Cowpeas	99.1	91		5.25	5.25				6.25		5.00	5.00			4.40	4.00
Soy beans	98.7	94	4.00	3.85	3.85	5.00	4.00	4.25	5.75	4.70	4.15				4.30	3.85
Seed grains:																
Seed corn	99.3	94		1.75		2.25	1.75	3.00	1.50	2.25	1.45			1.55	1.40
Seed wheat	98.8	94		1.85	1.75	1.60	1.75	1.40		1.65		1.75	1.95
Seed oats	98.6	95		.75	.95	.70	.75	.75	.80		.95	.75	.70
Seed barley	98.2	94		1.30	1.20	.95	.95	.95	1.00		.95	1.05	1.05
Seed rye	97.8	92		1.85		1.50	1.40	.95	1.10		1.40	1.50
Seed buckwheat	98.6	93	1.60	1.20	1.40	1.25	1.20	1.65	1.50		1.40	1.35

Cotton

Prices Advance.

Cotton prices advanced during the week March 10–15, and wide fluctuations again accompanied the movement. The average price of No. 5 or Middling cotton in 10 designated spot markets advanced a little more than ⅞¢ per lb., March future contracts advanced 100 points at New York and 72 points at New Orleans. The new crop future months advanced from 30 to 64 points on the two future exchanges.

Reports of further delay in farm work in the south due to wet and cold weather during a large part of the week, of the settlement early in the week of labor disputes in English cotton spinning centers, of difficulty experienced by buyers in obtaining some grades of spot cotton in the south due to dwindling supplies, and the report of a larger consumption of cotton during February than the trade had generally expected, were among the bullish factors in the market. The demand for cotton goods continued dull with prices about unchanged.

The average of the quotations for No. 5 cotton in 10 designated spot markets was 29.28¢ per lb. at the close of the week, compared with 28.46¢ on March 8, and 30.87¢ on March 17, 1923. March future contracts on the New York Cotton Exchange closed at 28.95¢, compared with 27.95¢ on the 8th. March future contracts at New Orleans closed at 29.50¢, compared with 28.78¢ on the 8th.

On March 14, the Bureau of the Census reported that American mills consumed 507,876 bales of cotton exclusive of linters during the month of February, compared with 576,644 bales in January and 566,805 bales in February, 1923. Stocks in consuming establishments were reported to be 1,578,272 bales on February 29, compared with 2,020,900 bales last year. The number of bales reported in independent warehouses and at compresses was 2,485,009, compared with 2,803,304 bales last year. The number of active cotton spindles during February was 32,683,786, compared with 35,304,423 for February, 1923.

Closing Future Prices on the Future Exchanges.

March 15, 1924, with Comparisons.

Month.	New York.					New Orleans.				
	Mar. 15, 1924.	Mar. 17, 1923.	Mar. 18, 1922.	Mar. 12, 1921.	Mar. 13, 1920.	Mar. 15, 1924.	Mar. 17, 1923.	Mar. 18, 1922.	Mar. 12, 1921.	Mar. 13, 1920.
	Cts.	Cts.	Cts.	Cts.	Cts.	Cts.	Cts.	Cts.	Cts.	Cts.
March	28.95	31.11	18.15	11.00	39.75	29.50	30.75	16.80	10.78	39.42
May	29.24	31.25	17.98	11.50	36.90	29.29	30.71	16.79	11.12	37.15
July	28.55	30.42	17.38	11.94	34.02	28.36	30.55	16.56	11.51	34.37
October	25.87	26.82	16.90	12.50	31.59	25.35	26.47	16.16	12.00	31.35
December	25.50	26.35	16.80	12.70	30.60	25.00	26.01	15.98	12.18	30.55

Daily Closing Quotations for No. 5 or Middling Spot Cotton at 10 Designated Spot Markets, Week of March 10–15, 1924, with Comparisons.

Market.	Mar. 10–15, 1924.						Mar. 12–17, 1923					
	Mon	Tue.	Wed.	Thu.	Fri.	Sat.	Mon	Tue.	Wed.	Thu.	Fri.	Sat.
	Cts.	Cts.	Cts.	Cts.	Cts.	Cts.	Cts.	Cts.	Cts.	Cts.	Cts.	Cts.
Norfolk	28.63	28.88	28.38	28.75	29.00	29.25	30.50	30.75	30.75	30.50	30.50	30.75
Augusta	29.00	29.31	28.81	29.25	29.38	29.63	30.44	30.81	30.81	30.56	30.63	30.81
Savannah	28.38	28.87	28.31	28.78	28.92	29.25	30.54	30.95	30.95	30.70	30.62	30.84
Montgomery	28.50	28.75	28.38	28.75	28.88	29.13	30.13	30.13	30.50	30.50	30.30	30.50
New Orleans	28.38	29.25	28.75	29.13	29.13	29.38	31.00	31.25	31.25	31.25	31.31	31.00
Memphis	29.00	29.50	29.00	29.00	29.00	29.25	31.00	31.00	31.25	31.25	31.31	31.00
Little Rock	28.75	29.00	28.75	29.00	29.00	29.25	30.25	30.50	30.50	30.50	30.50	30.50
Dallas	28.00	28.30	27.75	28.20	28.35	28.68	30.30	30.70	30.70	30.30	40.30	40.50
Houston	28.63	29.00	28.50	29.00	29.00	29.35	30.90	31.30	31.30	31.00	31.31	31.35
Galveston	28.25	29.25	28.75	29.15	29.35	29.90	31.20	31.50	31.50	31.05	31.05	31.25
Average	28.67	28.96	28.54	28.90	29.00	29.28	30.56	30.87	30.93	30.75	30.74	30.87

Quotations reported on March 14 for Pima American-Egyptian cotton f. o. b. New England mill points were as follows: No. 1 grade, 44¢ per lb.; No. 2, 43¢; No. 3, 42¢. A year ago Pima cotton on the same terms was quoted at 39¢ per lb. for No. 1 grade and 38¢ for No. 2.

Receipts at 10 Designated Spot Markets, August 1, 1923–March 14, 1924, and Stocks on March 14, 1924, with Comparisons.

(Compiled from commercial reports.)

Market.	Receipts.				Stocks.			
	Aug. 1, 1921–Mar. 17, 1922.	Aug. 1, 1922–Mar. 16, 1923.	Aug. 1, 1923–Mar. 14, 1924.	5-year average Aug. 1, 1918–19 to 1922–23.	Mar. 17, 1922.	Mar. 16, 1923.	Mar. 14, 1924.	5-year average Mar. 16, 1919–1923.
	1,000 bales.	1,000 bales.	1,000 bales.	1,000 bales.	1,000 bales.	1,000 bales.	1,000 bales.	1,000 bales.
Norfolk	269	251	369	247	129	84	72	100
Augusta	287	261	174	327	121	46	28	128
Savannah	533	343	332	627	129	46	37	137
Montgomery	44	53	48	54	28	9	13	22
New Orleans	846	1,134	1,055	1,017	243	160	150	325
Memphis	742	994	794	813	195	104	97	273
Little Rock	160	168	108	159	60	37	23	50
Dallas	158	58	118	79	41	7	3	20
Houston	2,204	2,599	3,317	2,024	240	147	189	256
Galveston	2,001	2,184	2,657	1,900	311	204	211	282
Total	7,244	8,047	8,982	7,247	1,497	844	828	1,595

Cotton Movement August 1, 1923–March 14, 1924, and Stocks March 14, 1924, with Comparisons.

(Compiled from commercial reports.)

	Aug. 1, 1913–Mar. 13, 1914.	Aug. 1, 1919–Mar. 12, 1920.	Aug. 1, 1920–Mar. 11, 1921.	Aug. 1, 1921–Mar. 17, 1922.	Aug. 1, 1922–Mar. 16, 1923.	Aug. 1, 1923–Mar. 14, 1924.	5-year average Mar. 16, 1918–19 to 1922–23.	Per cent this year is of 5-year average.
	1,000 bales.	1,000 bales.	1,000 bales.	1,000 bales.	1,000 bales.	1,000 bales.	1,000 bales.	Per cent.
Port receipts	9,254	5,891	4,567	4,408	5,026	5,804	4,699	123.5
Port stocks	876	1,317	1,416	1,039	674	685	1,151	59.5
Interior receipts	6,670	5,815	5,482	5,948	6,702	6,730	5,754	117.0
Interior stocks	724	1,240	1,703	1,262	801	697	1,307	53.3
Into sight	12,091	9,406	8,034	7,907	9,523	9,947	8,632	115.2
Northern spinners' takings	1,984	2,129	1,223	1,716	1,827	1,470	1,667	88.2
Southern spinners' takings	2,399	2,984	1,843	2,758	3,499	3,055	2,882	106.3
World's visible supply of American cotton	4,187	4,648	4,633	3,725	2,577	2,527	3,879	65.1

Exports of American Cotton.

August 1, 1923, to March 14, 1924, with Comparisons.

(Compiled from Government and commercial reports.)

To—	Aug. 1, 1913–Mar. 13, 1914.	Aug. 1, 1920–Mar. 11, 1921.	Aug. 1, 1921–Mar. 17, 1922.	Aug. 1, 1922–Mar. 16, 1923.	Aug. 1, 1923–Mar. 14, 1924.	4-year average Aug. 1– Mar. 16, 1919–20 to 1922–23.	Per cent this year is of 4-year average.
	Bales.	Bales.	Bales.	Bales.	Bales.	Bales.	Per cent.
Great Britain	2,690,504	1,193,173	1,061,523	1,197,565	1,460,582	1,475,894	99.0
France	979,105	422,281	491,094	525,914	575,539	472,689	121.8
Germany	2,342,876	703,160	962,041	711,950	938,888	669,658	140.2
Italy	355,790	369,447	271,787	383,057	417,798	353,677	118.1
Japan	309,071	229,093	678,568	415,741	469,099	463,784	101.4
China	538	8,294	71,436	13,700	20,550	24,381	84.3
Spain	214,420	191,524	209,532	195,659	154,917	181,857	85.2
Belgium	290,029	153,571	123,592	146,290	184,260	140,539	95.5
Canada [1]	107,587	106,729	118,502	141,888	107,455	123,946	86.7
Other countries	198,151	179,485	140,523	173,537	225,243	212,740	105.9
Total	7,544,829	3,616,697	4,116,598	3,904,801	4,504,931	4,118,462	109.4

[1] Exports to Canada are for the period Aug. 1 to Feb. 29.

Exports for the week ending March 14 amounted to 81,329 bales, compared with 100,354 bales the previous week, 98,962 bales for the corresponding week in 1923, and 114,267 bales for the week ending March 13, 1914.

Spot Quotations for No. 5 or Middling Upland Cotton at New York on March 14, for Each of the Past 32 Years.

	Cents.		Cents.		Cents.		Cents.
1893	9.00	1901	8.15	1909	9.85	1917	18.05
1894	7.50	1902	9.12	1910	15.20	1918	33.20
1895	6.00	1903	10.00	1911	14.65	1919	28.15
1896	7.69	1904	16.35	1912	10.75	1920	41.00
1897	7.25	1905	8.20	1913	12.50	1921	11.80
1898	6.12	1906	10.95	1914	13.25	1922	18.45
1899	6.38	1907	11.20	1915	8.80	1923	31.20
1900	9.75	1908	11.20	1916	12.00	1924	28.90

Stocks of American Cotton at European Ports, March 14, 1924, with Comparisons.

(Compiled from commercial reports.)

At—	Mar. 13, 1914.	Mar. 15, 1918.	Mar. 14, 1919.	Mar. 12, 1920.	Mar. 11, 1921.	Mar. 17, 1922.	Mar. 16, 1923.	Mar. 14, 1924.	5-year average Mar.16 1919-1923.
	1,000 bales.	1,000 bales.	1,000 bales.	1,000 bales.	1,000 bales.	1,000 bales.	1,000 bales.	1,000 bales.	1,000 bales.
Liverpool	967	293	301	855	632	538	448	455	555
Manchester	48	26	53	125	82	50	49	95	72
Continent	978	159	287	502	490	527	318	327	425
Total	1,993	478	641	1,482	1,204	1,115	815	877	1,052

Stocks of Egyptian cotton at Alexandria, Egypt, on March 14, were reported to be 204,000 bales of approximately 750 lbs. gross weight, compared with 275,000 bales on March 16, 1923. Stocks of Indian cotton at Bombay, India, on March 14, were reported to be 919,000 bales of approximately 400 lbs. gross weight, compared with 848,000 bales on March 16, 1923.

Premium Staple Cotton.

A fair demand for premium staple cotton was reported at both New Orleans and Memphis. Some of the sales reported in these markets during the week March 10–15, 1924, were:

New Orleans:	Cents.
No. 5 or Middling, 1 in.	30
No. 5 or Strict Middling, 1 in.	29.31
No. 3 or Good Middling, shy, 1 in.	30
No. 5 or Middling, shy, 1 to 1 1/8 ins.	28.95
No. 7 or Low Middling to No. 6 or Strict Low Middling, 1 1/8 ins.	28
No. 5 or Middling to No. 4 or Strict Middling, full 1 1/8 ins.	31
No. 5 or Middling, 1 1/8 to 1 1/4 ins.	30.50
No. 5 or Middling, 1 1/4 ins.	31
No. 6 or Strict Low Middling to No. 5 or Middling, 1 1/8 ins.	28.25
Memphis:	
No. 6 or Strict Low Middling, 1 1/8 ins.	29
No. 6 Spotted or Strict Low Middling Spotted, 1 1/8 ins.	29

Average Premiums for Staple Lengths of the Grade No. 5 or Middling, March 15, with Comparisons.

	New Orleans.			Memphis.		
	Mar. 15, 1924.	Mar. 17, 1923.	Mar. 18, 1922.	Mar. 15, 1924.	Mar. 17, 1923.	Mar. 18, 1922.
	Cents.	Cents.	Cents.	Cents.	Cents.	Cents.
No. 5 short staple	29.38	31.00	16.75	29.25	31.00	17.25
Length in inches.	Points.	Points.	Points.	Points.	Points.	Points.
1 1/16	100	75	200	50	50	125
1 1/8	175	150	450	125	75	475
1 3/16	275	225	650	[1]175	100	775
1 1/4	400	300	1,000	[1]175	300	1,075
1 5/16	500	375				
1 3/8	600	475				

[1] Nominal.

Spot Cotton Quotations for March 15, and Sales During Week of March 10–15, 1924.

Price of No. 5 or Middling spot cotton for March 15, the commercial differences in price between No. 5 and other grades of American Upland cotton at each of the 10 markets named, and average differences and prices for the corresponding day in previous years, together with the total number of bales sold during the week of March 10 10–15, 1924, in each of the markets and total for all the markets, with comparisons, as reported by the cotton exchanges.

Grade.	Norfolk.	Augusta.	Savannah.	Montgomery.	Memphis.	Little Rock.	Dallas.	Houston.	Galveston.	New Orleans.	Mar. 15, 1924.	Mar. 17, 1923.	Mar. 18, 1922.	Mar. 12, 1921.	Mar. 13, 1920.	Mar. 15, 1919.	Mar. 15, 1918.
														Average.			
White standards:	On.[1]	On.	On.	On.	On.	On.	On.	On.	On.	On.	On.	On.	On.	On.	On.	On.	On.
No. 1 or Middling Fair	175	162	225	125	200	175	175	225	185	181	91	198	313	333	209	126
No. 2 or Strict Good Middling	125	137	175	100	175	180	150	175	160	137	148	68	151	258	263	163	99
No. 3 or Good Middling	100	112	125	75	150	125	125	125	110	112	116	47	98	193	200	120	70
No. 4 or Strict Middling	50	75	75	50	75	75	75	75	75	75	76	51	100	113	64		37
No. 5 or Middling	29.25	29.63	29.25	29.13	29.25	29.25	28.65	29.35	29.65	29.38	29.28	30.87	17.19	11.01	40.63	27.12	32.68
	Off.[1]	Off.	Off.	Off.	Off.	Off.	Off.	Off.	Off.	Off.	Off.	Off.	Off.	Off.	Off.	Off.	Off.
No. 6 or Strict Low Middling	100	100	100	75	75	100	100	100	100	90	94	27	66	143	250	213	49
No. 7 or Low Middling	225	200	200	200	200	200	200	250	250	200	213	66	161	293	695	543	131
No. 8 or Strict Good Ordinary [2]	325	300	300	300	425	375	350	400	375	350	359	116	261	410	993	843	205
No. 9 or Good Ordinary [1]	450	400	400	400	575	500	450	550	525	500	475	170	364	515	1,260	1,053	281
Spotted:	On.	On.	On.	On.	On.	On.	On.	On.	On.	On.	On.						
No. 3 or Good Middling	50	50	63	50	25	50	50	25	60	50	47						
	Off.	Off.	Off.	Off.	Off.	Off.	Off.	Off.	Off.	Off.							
No. 4 or Strict Middling	Even	Even	Even	Even	25	25	25	25	25	Even	8						
No. 5 or Middling	75	100	75	75	100	75	100	100	Off 75	80	88						
No. 6 or Strict Low Middling [2]	175	175	200	175	175	175	175	200	250	235	175	194						
No. 7 or Low Middling [2]	275	300	300	300	300	275	300	400	395	300	315						
Yellow tinged:	On.	On.	On.	On.		On.	On.	On.	On.	On.	On.						
No. 2 or Strict Good Middling	13	38	13	13	Even	25	25	25	10	25	19						
	Off.	Off.	Off.	Off.	Off.	Off.	Off.	Off.	Off.	Off							
No. 3 or Good Middling	25	Even	25	25	25	25	25	50	15	25	24	Even.	23	80	193	203	8
No. 4 or Strict Middling	75	100	75	63	75	50	75	100	50	75	74	38	100	173	310	307	36
No. 5 or Middling	175	200	175	150	125	150	175	200	175	170	170	93	200	285	470	473	69
No. 6 or Strict Low Middling [2]	300	300	300	275	225	250	250	400	320	250	287	138	299	423	690	708	116
No. 7 or Low Middling [2]	400	400	400	400	375	350	325	550	490	375	407	[1]188	389	545	1,008	988	177
Light Yellow Stained:																	
No. 3 or Good Middling	75	100	75	75	75	75	75	100	90	100	84						
No. 4 or Strict Middling [2]	125	150	150	125	125	125	150	175	150	175	143						
No. 5 or Middling [2]	200	200	200	200	175	175	225	300	225	250	215						
Yellow Stained:																	
No. 3 or Good Middling	113	150	150	125	100	125	100	200	165	150	138	66	196	240	460	465	63
No. 4 or Strict Middling [1]	175	200	200	175	150	150	175	150	300	200	198	121	279	338	608	608	106
No. 5 or Middling [2]	225	250	250	250	225	200	400	300	380	268	171	375	443	745	765	142	
Gray:																	
No. 3 or Good Middling	50	38	35	38 On 25	50	50	50 On 10	50	33								
No. 4 or Strict Middling [1]	100	88	85	88 Off 50	100	100	100 Off 25	100	84								
No. 5 or Middling [2]	150	150	150	138	125	150	150	150	150	146							
Blue Stained:																	
No. 3 or Good Middling [2]	125	125	125	113	125	125	150	90	150	125	95	221	308	575	610	64
No. 4 or Strict Middling [2]	175	175	175	163	200	125	175	200	200	174	133	303	403	683	713	111
No. 5 or Middling [2]	325	250	250	238	275	225	250	250	230	300	261	173	396	480	820	855	152
Sales for week, bales	594	429	416	59	2,450	882	4,737	2,248	12,694	4,253	[3]28,762	[3]19,944	[3]59,270	[3]48,350	[3]65,300	[3]54,845	[3]42,072

[1] The differences are stated in terms of points or hundredths of a cent per pound. By "On" is meant that the stated number of points is to be added to the price of No. 5 and by "Off" is meant that the stated number of points is to be subtracted from the price of No. 5.

[2] These grades are not tenderable on future contracts made subject to section 5 of the United States cotton futures act, as amended, on the future exchanges at New York and New Orleans.

[3] Total sales. Sales from Aug. 1, 1923 to Mar. 15, 1924, amounted to 3,455,048 bales, compared with 3,283,540 bales during the corresponding period in 1922–23 and 2,465,790 bales in 1921–22.

Foreign Crops and Markets

Progress in British Home Bacon Trade.

The substantial progress being made in the extension of the British home bacon trade is called attention to in a recent number of The Agricultural Gazette. (British) which points out that three additional cooperative farmer-owned bacon factories, drawing supplies from fifteen counties, have been established in the last 18 months all of them entirely upon the initiative of English pig producers themselves.

It is stated that throughout the country there is a growing belief in the possibilities of profitable pig rearing. Many farmers are largely increasing their herds, and others who have not previously kept hogs are now starting to do so. The great breed societies are more active than ever before, the entries in the pig classes at shows are increasing, the country is deluged with all types of pig foods and dry feeders, while the extra space being devoted to all questions affecting the industry in the agricultural press bears witness to a remarkable and widespreading interest. The existing cooperative societies have already formed a central council to further their interests, both financially and administratively, and there is every prospect of an incorporated federation emanating from it.

In June, 1922, there were in operation three farmers' cooperative bacon factories, drawing supplies from seven English counties. To-day six factories are drawing from 15 counties, and there seems to be every possibility that by the end of this year there will be 10 societies covering 24 counties, each situated in the center of a pig population of not less than 120,000.

Farmer shareholders to the number of 4,500 have invested in factories up to the present time approximately $800,000. The turnover in farmer-cured bacon by the end of 1924, if present plans mature, will amount to around $8,500,000 at present rates of exchange.

The gazette also goes on to state that the indications are that an increase in English hog production is to be looked for, notwithstanding that a few of the more timid farmers are likely to be influenced by a drop in prices such as has occurred in recent months. This view of the situation, however, seems open to some doubt, in light of the fact that English production before the war followed closely the cycle of hog production in the United States, which was much influenced by the prices farmers obtained for hogs. Whether the new cooperative societies have yet gained a strong enough foothold to maintain English hog production and even increase it in the face of existing low prices is a question of considerable interest to the hog industry everywhere, and one that remains to be answered.

Possibilities for Growth of Hog Industry in Yugoslavia.

An offer relating to the starting of factories in Yugoslavia for preparing and canning pork, and the formation of a company to develop the export of such products to Great Britain and Switzerland, has recently been received from British and Swiss capitalists by the Ministry of Commerce at Belgrade, according to a report to the British Trade Journal by its correspondent at Fiume.

The possibilities for pork production in Yugoslavia suggested by the report are well borne out by the facts. The country is well supplied with hogs, and exported in pre-war years to Austria-Hungary and other near-by countries. It is rich in natural grazing resources and corn and other feeds for the support of the hog industry are fairly cheap and abundant. Experts go so far as to state that if the Yugoslavian hog and packing-house industry were properly organized, the country would prove a serious competitor with American hog products in the markets of western Europe.

Although the native pig is not suitable for slaughter for the English bacon trade, because of its coarse flesh, there are enough pigs of English breeds in the country to enable the production and export of bacon when packing and transportation facilities are increased. The native hog, while not satisfactory for bacon, is successfully being fattened for lard production and for export to Austria, Germany and other neighboring countries, either alive or as fat pork. The total number of hogs, according to reliable estimates, increased from 3,373,000 in 1921 to 4,887,000 in 1922 and the number of either or both types of can be increased readily if their production is given any real encouragement.

The French Wheat Situation.

France will not have to resort to further purchases of wheat from abroad before the next harvest if the farmers can be prevailed upon to market the supplies of wheat they are now holding, according to a statement made by the president of the Paris Grain Dealers' Syndicate, and published in Le Matin on January 25, 1924. France is now assured of a total supply for the season of over 367,000,000 bushels, while the annual requirements amount to only 331,000,000 bushels, he says. The French farmer, however, will have to place his wheat on the market and an appeal is being made to his patriotism to release his wheat.

The official figures for the 1923 harvest in France, he says, are 286,000,000 bushels. The quantity carried over from the preceding crop year is placed at 22,000,000 bushels. Imports from August 1 to December 31 totaled 26,000,000 bushels. The quantity already purchased for delivery during January, February, March, and April of 1924, he says, amounts to 15,000,000 bushels. The quantity saved by increasing the milling percentage will total 7,000,000 bushels, while the quantity saved by the incorporation of wheat substitutes in the flour will amount to 11,000,000 bushels. These figures allow a total supply for the 1923–24 crop year of 367,000,000 bushels, or an excess of over 36,000,000 bushels above actual requirements.

Cultivation of Yeoman Wheat in England.

The cultivation of "Yeoman" wheat in the United Kingdom is meeting with a fair degree of success according to a report submitted by the consul general, Robert P. Skinner, at London. A number of British farmers have been experimenting with this wheat for years. "Yeoman" wheat possesses the free-milling characteristics of Manitoba wheats and the flour yielded is just sufficiently strong to produce a salable loaf without being blended with imported wheats. The wheat is not strong enough, however, to take the place of Manitoba. Hard in the blends millers now use for the production of flour for breadmaking. In districts where "Yeoman" wheat is available in quantity millers have found that they could profitably make use of 80% of it in their mixtures. The significant factor is that British growers are beginning to show a disinclination toward accepting lower prices for their grain on the grounds that their grain can only be used with difficulty in the mills. They are, therefore, demanding better prices from millers for the superior grain they are now offering.

Australasian Wool Exports.

Exports of wool from Australia and New Zealand from July 1, 1923, to January 31, 1924, amounted to only 1,277,000 bales of from 330 to 350 lbs. each, as compared with 1,665,000 bales during the corresponding seven months of the 1922–23 season, according to information cabled by Dalgety & Co. (Ltd.), from Melbourne, Australia. This represents a decrease of 388,000 bales, due chiefly to the decrease in exports from Australia, which amounted to only 1,029,000 bales this year as compared with 1,413,000 bales during the first seven months of the previous season. Exports from New Zealand totaled 248,000 bales as against 252,000 bales the year before.

B. A. W. R. A. Stocks Practically Exhausted.

The surplus stocks of crossbred wool held by the British Australian Wool Realization Association have dwindled to a point at which they no longer influence the market, the supply remaining on hand on February 1, 1924, amounting to only 130,290 bales as compared with 209,617 bales on January 1, 1924, a decrease of over 79,000 bales. This balance of 130,000 bales is all that remains of nearly 3,000,000 bales held by the British Ministry of Munitions in 1920.

Wool Imports at Three Ports.

Imports of wool through the port of Philadelphia during the week ending March 15, 1924, amounted to 764 bales, weighing 293,546 lbs., valued at $71,801, imports through the port of Boston amounted to 7,096 bales, weighing 2,605,450 lbs., valued at $1,129,003 and imports through the port of New York amounted to 1,599 bales, weighing 865,127 lbs., valued at $18,750,586.

CPSIA information can be obtained
at www.ICGtesting.com
Printed in the USA
BVHW04s1042210918
528173BV00023B/2031/P